ISO 14000
A Guide to the New Environmental Management Standards

Tom Tibor with Ira Feldman

IRWIN
Professional Publishing®

Chicago • London • Singapore

This publication is designed to provide accurate and authoritative information in regard to the subject matter covered. It is sold with the understanding that neither the author nor the publisher is engaged in rendering legal, accounting, or other professional service. If legal advice or other expert assistance is required, the services of a competent professional person should be sought.

From a Declaration of Principles jointly adopted by a Committee of the American Bar Association and a Committee of Publishers.

Irwin Professional Book Team

Publisher: *Wayne McGuirt*
Senior sponsoring editor: *Cynthia A. Zigmund*
Marketing manager: *J. D. Kinney*
Project editor: *Jane Lightell*
Production supervisor: *Pat Frederickson/Carol Klein*
Prepress buyer: *Jon Christopher*
Compositor: *David Corona Design*
Typeface: *11/13 Times Roman*
Printer: *Buxton Skinner Printing Company*

◥▼ **Times Mirror**
Ⓜ **Higher Education Group**

Library of Congress Cataloging-in-Publication Data
Tibor, Tom.
    ISO 14000 : a guide to the new environmental management standards
/ Tom Tibor with Ira Feldman.
        p.   cm.
    Includes index.
    ISBN 0-7863-0523-1
    1. ISO 9000 Series Standards.   2. Environmental protection—
—Standards.   I. Feldman, Ira.   II. Title.
TS156.6T53 1996
658.5'62—dc20   95–37280

*This book is dedicated
to my mother and father,
Susan and Alfred Tibor.*

Contents

Preface

This book is a snapshot of a moving train—the ongoing development of the ISO 14000 series of environmental management standards. The authors have participated in the inner workings of this process at the national and international level. Thus, the information is as current and accurate as possible. This book is a comprehensive preview of standards that are in development, not a detailed implementation manual.

The book has a broad audience. It is primarily directed at environmental managers and other environmental personnel in companies. It is also useful for managers in other areas of the organization, such as marketing, and research and development. It will also be of interest to anyone concerned about environmental management and how ISO 14000 will fit into the overall trend to improve the environmental performance of industrial operations. This includes government officials, members of nongovernmental organizations, industry associations, and other groups.

Contents

The goals of this book are to:

- Trace the background and development of the ISO 14000 series of environmental management standards.
- Describe the elements of each standard in development, including environmental management systems, environmental auditing, environmental performance evaluation, life cycle assessment, and environmental labeling.
- Describe other important related developments, such as the European Union's Eco-Management and Audit Scheme (EMAS).
- Explore the regulatory community's possible use of the ISO 14000 standards and the role of ISO 14000 in international trade.
- Trace the outlines of the probable ISO 14000 registration process.

- Provide some preliminary orientation for managers who may be charged with implementing an environmental management system in their organizations.

How to use the book

The primary focus of this book is on the main standard that will be used by organizations for internal use and for registration (certification) purposes—ISO 14001. This standard is, as of fall 1995, in Draft International Standard (DIS) form, which is only one step away from publication as an international standard. The auditing standards have also reached the same phase. The others in the ISO 14000 series, however, are not nearly as far in their development. In addition, the registration (certification) process has not yet begun. Therefore, some of the discussion in this book is general and necessarily speculative.

To the greatest extent possible, the authors focus on the key concepts in the standards, those that are likely to remain in the final versions. Keep in mind that the discussion in this book paraphrases the requirements of some of the standards. By far the greatest specificity is in the discussion of ISO 14001 specification standard. No explanation in a book of this type is ever a substitute, however, for acquiring copies of the actual standards and examining them closely.

Conventions

There are some terms used in this book that should be explained to avoid confusion. First, "ISO 14000" is itself confusing. In one sense, it is a shorthand phrase that actually refers to the ISO 14000 series of environmental management standards, of which there are already over two dozen in development. ISO 14000 or the ISO 14000 series is often used simply for conciseness and readability.

Second, until recently, ISO 14000 also referred to a specific standard in the series, the ISO 14000 guidance standard. The number of this standard has been changed to ISO 14004.

Third, the phrase "ISO 14000 registration (certification)" is commonly used even though the actual standard used in the registration process is the specification standard—ISO 14001. Registration refers to the process whereby an independent third party audits the organization's environmental management system to evaluate whether it conforms to the requirements of the ISO 14001 specification standard.

Registration is one of several ways to implement ISO 14000. A company can develop an environmental management system and self-declare that it complies with ISO 14001 requirements. Or it may have its environmental management system audited by a customer as part of a contractual arrangement. Thus the phrase "ISO 14000 implementation" need not automatically imply ISO 14000 registration. Organizations can use the standards internally without planning to seek third-party registration.

To dispel confusion, this book will use ISO 14000 only in the context of general discussions, such as "the ISO 14000 process." References to specific standards will always use the specific term (i.e., ISO/DIS 14001) and the same will hold true regarding the registration process (i.e., ISO 14001 registration).

Finally, the terms *accreditation, certification,* and *registration* can cause confusion. To clarify the meanings, the Conformity Assessment Committee of the International Organization for Standardization (CASCO), in its *ISO/IEC Guide 2: General Terms and Their Definitions Concerning Standardization and Certification,* defines the terms as follows:

Accreditation: Procedure by which an authoritative body gives formal recognition that a body or person is competent to carry out specific tasks.

Certification: Procedure by which a third party gives written assurance that a product, process, or service conforms to specific requirements.

Registration: Procedure by which a body indicates relevant characteristics of a product, process, or service, or particulars of a body or person, and then includes or registers the product, process, or service in an appropriate publicly available list.

Although certification and registration are slightly different in these definitions, they are synonymous in common usage. The United States favors the term *registration* while the international community prefers *certification.* This book generally uses *registration,* but because it has been written for an international audience, occasionally it uses *certification.*

Some readers may be familiar with the ISO 9000 series of quality management and quality assurance standards. Since the development of ISO 14000 originated, in part, with ISO 9000, this book occasionally uses analogies from the ISO 9000 arena to assist in explaining some concepts. This is done for illustration purposes; it is not meant to imply that ISO 9000 implementation and/or registration is a prerequisite for ISO 14000 implementation.

Tom Tibor   **Ira Feldman**
Arlington, Virginia   *Washington, D.C.*

I

ENVIRONMENTAL MANAGEMENT
A New Paradigm

Chapter One

Introduction

If you're an environmental manager, you're probably familiar with scenarios such as these:

- Management okays the new construction of a plant without fully considering the requirements of operating permits.
- The purchasing department shifts from a domestic to a foreign chemical supplier. However, the new chemical does not meet regulatory requirements.
- Downsizing at a plant proceeds, but no one is charged with reassessing key environmental responsibilities.
- A change in a materials specification requires a new Material Safety Data Sheet, which hasn't been developed by either the technical, marketing, or regulatory affairs departments.
- Management issues lofty policy statements lauding environmental improvement but does not accompany them with resources and personnel.
- The local community is concerned about the plant's discharges to a local stream but hasn't developed an effective communication program to ease the community's concerns.
- In general, the environmental staff is too busy putting out today's fires to find time to prevent those that may occur tomorrow.

What do these situations have in common? To a large extent, they are system failures. Either a good environmental management system doesn't exist, or if it does, it's not working as well as it should.

There's a set of standards just around the corner that may well change things. Known as the ISO 14000 series, it will affect every aspect of a company's management of its environmental responsibilities: how it performs environmental auditing; how it measures environmental performance; how it makes credible claims for its products; the way it analyzes the life cycle of its products and processes; and the way it reports environmental information to its employees and the public.

In short, the ISO 14000 standards will help any organization address environmental issues in a systematic way and thereby improve its environmental performance.

The ISO 14000 standards are being developed by Technical Committee 207 (TC 207) of the International Organization for Standardization (ISO) to provide organizations worldwide with a common approach to environmental management. Just as the ISO 9000 quality standards were developed to address quality management, the ISO 14000 standards are emerging to address a similar need in the environmental area.

WHAT IS AN ENVIRONMENTAL MANAGEMENT SYSTEM?

The ISO 14000 standards describe the basic elements of an effective environmental management system, routinely referred to by the acronym EMS. These elements include creating an environmental policy, setting objectives and targets, implementing a program to achieve those objectives, monitoring and measuring its effectiveness, correcting problems, and reviewing the system to improve it and overall environmental performance.

An effective environmental management system can help a company manage, measure, and improve the environmental aspects of its operations. It can lead to more efficient compliance with mandatory and voluntary environmental requirements. It can help companies effect a culture change as environmental management practices are incorporated into its overall business operations.

The ISO 14000 standards are based on a simple equation: better environmental management will lead to better environmental performance, increased efficiency, and a greater return on investment.

MANAGEMENT SYSTEMS AND TOOLS

The work of ISO's TC 207 encompasses standards in the following areas:

- Environmental management systems (EMS).
- Environmental auditing (EA).
- Environmental performance evaluation (EPE).

- Environmental labeling.
- Life cycle assessment (LCA).
- Environmental aspects in product standards (EAPS).
- Terms and definitions.

These areas fall into two general groups, as shown in Figure 1–1. The EMS, EA, and EPE standards are used to evaluate the organization. The EMS standards provide the basic framework for the management system. Environmental auditing and environmental performance evaluation are management tools that play a critical role in the successful implementation of the environmental management system.

The work in the areas of labeling, life cycle assessment, and environmental aspects in product standards will also play an important role in the environmental arena. The emphasis in these areas, however, is on the evaluation and analysis of product and process characteristics.

FIGURE 1–1
The ISO 14000 Series of Environmental Management Standards

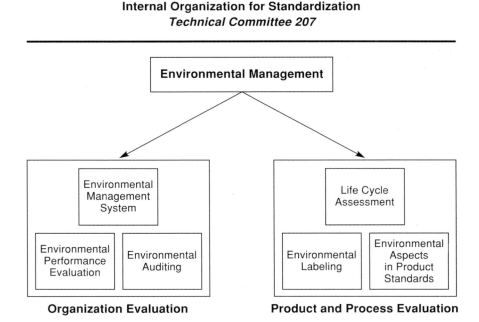

This book is organized according to the classification shown in Figure 1–1. Part I sets the context for environmental management and the work of TC 207; Part II looks at the organizational evaluation standards (EMS, EA, and EPE); Part III describes the work in the product evaluation area; and Part IV focuses on the implementation of the environmental management system and registration (certification) issues.

System, Not Performance

One key point that will facilitate an understanding of the standards is this: The ISO 14000 standards are *process*—not *performance*—standards. That is, ISO 14000 does not tell companies what environmental performance they must achieve. Instead, it offers companies the building blocks for a system that will help them achieve their own goals. The basic assumption is that better environmental management will lead indirectly to better environmental performance. The standards being developed by TC 207 do not, therefore, set performance levels or rates of improvement, nor do they prescribe specific goals, objectives, or policies.

One reason for this approach is that there are many different points of view on what constitutes good environmental management and performance. In part, this relates to diverse technologies to meet company objectives. That's why the goal of standards such as the ISO 14000 series is to lay a common foundation for more uniform, efficient, and effective environmental management worldwide. The result will be increased confidence among all stakeholders involved that the process put in place by a company will lead to better compliance with laws and other requirements and to high levels of environmental performance.

THE PACE OF DEVELOPMENT

Some of the standards in the ISO 14000 series are already in the form of Draft International Standards (DIS), one step away from published International Standards (IS). The EMS standards and the auditing standards could be published by mid-1996. Most standards developed at the international level take five years to reach publication. ISO 14000 has been in development less than two years. Why so fast?

Response to Proliferation

One reason is the growing proliferation of environmental management standards and voluntary initiatives. These are being developed by industry and government. At least a dozen countries have EMS standards, including the United Kingdom's BS 7750 and, in the United States, the NSF International's NSF 110 EMS standard.

Regional trading blocs such as the European Union have developed the Eco-Management and Audit Scheme regulation. Industry associations have developed codes of practice, such as the US Chemical Management Association's Responsible Care program; the Global Environmental Management Initiative's (GEMI) Environmental Self Assessment Program, and many others.

Without a common international standard, companies would be forced to deal with dozens of separate and potentially incompatible systems for every country in which they do business. This can increase the cost of doing business and pose trade barriers.

Environmental Stewardship and Accountability

The ISO 14000 standards setting activity is set against a broader tapestry. Generally speaking, the standards are developing quickly partly in response to the growing pressure on companies to demonstrate better environmental stewardship and accountability. Pressure is coming from the government, the public, stockholders, financial institutions, environmental groups, and others. With each passing month, anecdotal evidence of the trend accumulates.

Greener Products

As consumers, the public is also beginning to play a role. Consumer demand is increasing for green products, and companies are responding by taking a closer look at all environmental aspects of product design, production, packaging, distribution, and disposal. The investing public is taking a closer look at a company's environmental operations as a factor in its profitability.

For these reasons and others, ISO 14000 may well have an explosive impact on the global marketplace. Although designed as a voluntary standard, it could become a de facto market-driven requirement for companies both domestic and international. ISO 14000 may well become a company's global passport to doing business. That's why proactive companies are already paying close attention to ISO 14000.

REASONS TO IMPLEMENT ISO 14000

First, there are strategic reasons to get involved. Increasingly, as we've discussed, there is a worldwide trend to focus on better environmental management. Environmental management has gone from an add-on function to an integral part of business operations. For many proactive companies, environmental management has become strategy-driven, not compliance-driven. ISO 14000 will provide a broad framework for implementing strategic environmental management.

Increasing Use of Voluntary Standards

There's also an emphasis on the use of voluntary international standards. The General Agreement on Tariffs and Trade (GATT) officially favors the use of international standards in its agreement on Technical Barriers to Trade (TBT).

This trend has been integrated into national policies. In the United States, for example, it's government policy to reference international standards whenever possible.[1]

The use of international standards can help level the international playing field. In countries with high compliance costs due to stringent regulations, companies can achieve more efficient compliance. In countries where compliance costs may be lower, due partly to a less stringent regulatory system, ISO 14000 may demand more of a commitment to effective environmental management.

Reduce Multiplicity/Duplication

The acceptance of a single international environmental standard can reduce the number of environmental audits conducted by customers, regulators, or registrars. By avoiding conflicting requirements, multinational corporations could reduce the cost of multiple inspections, certifications, and other conflicting requirements.

De Facto Requirement

Implementing an EMS that complies with ISO 14000 requirements and achieving third-party registration may well become a de facto requirement to do business. Foreign customers may require US suppliers to be ISO 14000 registered. This requirement could affect the ability of US companies to sell their products globally.

Even if ISO 14000 remains a purely voluntary standard, market pressure may drive registration. The pressure will not just be on large multinational companies but also on smaller companies that are part of the supplier chain. The trend is for companies to want to deal with environmentally responsible companies. ISO 14000 itself requires that organizations establish and maintain procedures related to the environmental aspects of goods and services that they use and communicate these procedures and requirements to suppliers and contractors. Since ISO 14000 registration is one way to demonstrate that a company has a system in place to achieve environmental performance objectives, companies may come to expect ISO 14000 registration of their suppliers and subcontractors.

Government Adoption

Another key player in the ISO 14000 movement could be government. Governments worldwide are looking at the role that ISO 14000 can play in their regulatory systems, their enforcement procedures, and their procurement policies. (See Box.)

In the European Union, ISO 14000 certification may satisfy the EMS requirements of the Eco-Management and Audit Scheme regulation. This is a voluntary scheme open to industrial sites in Europe that requires extensive EMS and auditing systems to be in place. (See Chapter 5 for an overview of EMAS.)

Many other countries around the world are looking at ISO 14000, either to encourage their industries to get involved or to actually integrate the standard into their regulatory system in some fashion.

Governments in developed countries with strict environmental regulations are interested in ISO 14000 as a useful alternative to complex and expensive "command and control" regulations.

Other nations, especially in the developing countries, are looking at the use of ISO 14000 as a way to enhance regulatory systems that are either nonexistent or weak in their environmental performance requirements. In these countries, ISO 14000 registration may be an alternative method to achieve environmental goals.

In any case, even if the international standard isn't integrated into regulations, it may nevertheless influence national regulations by establishing a standard of care—a new level of expectations for EMS programs—that may guide the development of national regulations.

It may also affect enforcement policies. In the United States, the Environmental Protection Agency (EPA), the Department of Justice (DOJ), the Department of Energy (DOE), and the Department of Commerce (DOC) are among several agencies that are monitoring the ISO 14000 process and its role in regulation and enforcement.

Several countries are also considering giving preference in procurement contracts to companies that install an EMS that conforms to ISO 14000 requirements.[2]

Government and ISO 14000

Governments worldwide are closely monitoring the ISO 14000 process. The UK's Ministry of Defense may require potential vendors to achieve EMS registration, and it may offer favorable treatment regarding permit issuance to companies that comply with the UK's BS 7750 EMS standard. In the Netherlands, thousands of Dutch companies have agreed to implement EMS systems as part of government-industry covenants that supplement existing laws and regulations. The Dutch government may use EMS registration to issue permits and check compliance among regulated companies.

ISO 14000 registration can assist governments in using regulatory resources more efficiently. Germany, for example, is looking at the role ISO 14000 can play in deregulatory efforts and in simplification of its permitting procedures. Governments in South America—for example, those in Brazil, Argentina, and Chile—may apply pressure on companies in key sectors such as petroleum, mining, auto manufacturing, and the paper and pulp industries to implement ISO 14000. The same holds true for many Asian countries, many of whom have participated actively in the standards development process.

US Government and ISO 14000

In the United States, many government agencies are monitoring the standards activities. The Department of Energy (DOE) may require major DOE contractors to put into place an environmental management system along the lines of ISO 14001 by 1997. The ISO 14000 standards may also play a role in the US government's procurement policies related to environmentally preferable products.[3]

The Environmental Protection Agency (EPA) has been participating actively in the standards drafting process. The EPA recognizes that ISO 14000 is a private-sector effort and thus, it is not at present considering the adoption of the ISO 14000 standards as a possible regulatory requirement. The EPA will likely find ISO 14000 to be a useful tool in its voluntary programs, as described below. In general, US industry would not welcome ISO 14000 implementation and/or third-party registration as a regulatory mandate.

As discussed in Appendix C, the EPA has developed policies that mitigate the enforcement response for companies performing environmental auditing and offer incentives for voluntary disclosure. In general, the EPA will follow the general US government trend to take into account a company's compliance assurance programs in its responses to violations. This is also true for the Department of Justice and the US Sentencing Commission.

As in other countries with complex regulatory schemes, the EPA is looking for ways to move away from its purely command and control posture and toward preventive approaches such as ISO 14000. The EPA anticipates more reliance by companies on independent auditing and self-certification as the primary way to prevent environmental problems and ensure regulatory compliance. One benefit to the EPA and to regulatory bodies in other countries that pursue the same strategy is greater regulatory efficiency; governments can ease oversight of environmental "good actors" and direct their attention to serious violators.

According to the EPA, possible uses of the ISO 14000 standard could include the following:

- Reduction of penalties and recognition of due diligence in complying with regulations.
- Special public recognition of some kind for ISO 14000–registered companies.

(Continued)

(Continued)

- A schedule of fewer routine inspections and regulatory audits in exchange for EMS implementation.
- Faster permitting procedures.
- Adoption by companies in place of compliance penalties in consent decree negotiations.
- Reduced or streamlined reporting and monitoring burdens and less paperwork.
- Some role in government supplier requirements, such as the environmentally preferable products orders.

ISO 14000 in voluntary programs. The ISO 14000 standards are likely to play a role in voluntary programs to encourage companies to comply with regulations and improve environmental performance.

One such program is the EPA's Environmental Leadership Program (ELP), a one-year pilot project launched in March 1995 at 12 facilities. The basic concept of the program is to encourage companies to go beyond compliance by testing innovative management techniques such as environmental auditing, pollution prevention, and EMS programs. Another purpose of the program is to test criteria for auditing and for certification of voluntary compliance programs to standards such as ISO 14000.[4]

The program will provide the EPA with more information about the elements of a state-of-the-art EMS program. If successful, the criteria developed through the pilot projects could lead to reduced inspections and public recognition for companies or agencies with successful compliance programs. Similar programs are being developed at the state level.

Satisfy Stakeholder Interests

Companies are increasingly concerned with satisfying the expectations of a broad range of stakeholders, including investors, the public, and environmental groups. ISO 14000 registration can satisfy the public's need for corporate accountability. Companies with ISO 14000–registered EMS programs can provide confidence to the public that they are complying with regulations and continually improving their environmental management systems. ISO 14000 registration can demonstrate an organization's commitment and credibility regarding environmental issues. It demonstrates compliance not only with existing regulations but also with a publicly declared policy such as the ICC Charter.

Lower Insurance Rates and Better Access to Capital

Implementing an effective EMS can provide future savings in the form of lower insurance rates and better access to capital. Insurance companies will be more willing to issue coverage for pollution incidents if the company requesting coverage has a proven environmental management system in place. Some large institutional investors such as pension funds have begun to make investment decisions based on a corporation's environmental track record. This ties environmental management to future stock performance.

Internal Benefits

The discussion so far has focused on external pressures and benefits. What will ISO 14000 implementation do for an organization internally?

On a practical level, an ISO 14000 type of EMS program is likely to lead to cost savings through better management of the environmental aspects of an organization's operations.

To the extent that noncompliance with regulations is caused by systems deficiencies, implementing an EMS can reduce the number of noncompliances and increase overall operating efficiency. It can lead to waste reduction, pollution prevention, substitution of less toxic chemicals and other materials, less energy usage, cost savings through recycling, and other such programs. It can facilitate obtaining operating permits and other authorizations.

ISO 14000 can provide a mechanism for controlling existing management methods, integrating fragmented systems, or creating systems if none exist. It can help a company systematically monitor and measure its compliance status. It can help in training employees regarding their role in environmental protection and improvement. An effective EMS can integrate existing management systems to reduce costs and system duplication.

Pollution Prevention

ISO 14000 acceptance worldwide will provide more incentives to initiate pollution prevention activities. A company with an ISO 14000 system can gain some breathing room—instead of constantly putting out fires, it can prevent them from occurring in the first place. An effective EMS program analyzes the cause of noncompliances and builds prevention into the company's overall operations.

The key to prevention is successfully integrating environmental issues, business strategy, and operations. Prevention cuts costs by reducing the use of materials and energy, while end-of-pipe controls only save money from the avoidance of fines and penalties due to noncompliance.

Achieve Environmental Excellence

An effective EMS will help organizations implement their commitment to environmental excellence. The basic elements of ISO 14000 do not constitute an environmental excellence program in and of themselves; however, they are the foundation—the building blocks—for such a program. Stakeholder pressure, marketplace competition, and encouragement and recognition by government agencies are providing incentives for more companies to achieve environmental excellence.

On the broadest scale, better environmental management can protect human health and the environment from the impacts of industrial activity. An EMS can help an organization balance economic and environmental interests. It brings environmental issues into day-to-day decision-making processes. In short, ISO 14000 marries environmental management to business management.

CONCERNS AND CAVEATS

The benefits just discussed shouldn't disguise the concerns, caveats, and potential pitfalls in the ISO 14000 movement. In many cases, these are the flip side of the benefits.

Increased Costs

Implementing a comprehensive environmental management system can be expensive. Costs are especially critical for small and medium-size enterprises (SMEs), many of whom already have problems meeting environmental obligations. Depending on the definition of small business, anywhere from 75 to 90 percent of world industry is performed by SMEs. For small companies, the time and cost of ISO 14000 registration may be too high a price to play the game and thus the standard may pose a trade barrier for such companies.

The standards drafters claim that the ISO 14000 standards take into account the problems of industries in lesser developed countries and those of small companies. The ISO 14001 specification standard posits a gradual, baseline approach to managing environmental systems. Thus, a company need not start with the most sophisticated EMS. Implementing ISO 14000 effectively in SMEs, however, will remain an important challenge for the ISO 14000 movement.

Possible Nontariff Trade Barriers

International standards can facilitate a common industrial language, provide consumer confidence, and promote product safety. Standards can also encourage trade by making it more efficient and by simplifying testing and certification requirements for products and processes. Used improperly, however, standards can hinder worldwide trade by creating technical (nontariff) trade barriers.

A major goal of TC 207 is to facilitate trade and minimize trade barriers by leveling the playing field. But the standard could have the opposite effect and lead to imposing the requirements and management systems of advanced industrial nations on developing countries, requirements they lack the knowledge and resources to meet.

ISO 14000 and Trade Barriers

The work of TC 207 does not exist in a vacuum but rather in a highly competitive international economy. This economy comprises nations at widely different levels of economic development, with varying degrees of environmental regulation. In this context, the aim of ISO 14000 is worldwide adoption by industry, improvements in environmental performance, and avoidance of trade barriers. ISO 14000 implementation, however, could actually create trade barriers. How could this happen?

Regulatory adoption by a country. ISO 14000 is a voluntary standard, and ISO 14001 registration is a voluntary scheme. Therefore, ISO 14000 does not create any official trade barrier as recognized by international agreements such as the General Agreement of Tariffs and Trade (GATT) in its agreement on Technical Barriers to Trade (TBT). If a country makes ISO 14000 registration a regulatory requirement for all companies doing business within its borders, however, this raises a potential barrier to foreign companies that find it difficult, for various reasons, to meet the requirements of the standard. This might apply especially if the foreign

(Continued)

(Continued)

company facing the barrier is a subcontractor or vendor to a company located in the country with the requirement. Foreign suppliers who want to get contract awards but who cannot meet the "green" requirements of their customers, for whatever reason, may encounter market access barriers.

Barrier to developing countries. Requirements for ISO 14000 registration, whether government or marketplace mandated, can disadvantage developing nations. Even though ISO 14000 registration can be an opportunity for companies in developing nations to demonstrate effective environmental management, if ISO 14000 registration is expensive and the standards are too prescriptive to meet developing nations will be disadvantaged.

Another barrier faced by many countries is the lack of a registration and accreditation infrastructure. This may require companies in these countries to seek registrations from registrars in other nations, again potentially driving up costs and creating trade barriers.

Voluntary or Mandated?

The basic purpose of a voluntary consensus standard is just that—to stay voluntary. Another trade barrier issue arises if the standard becomes a regulatory mandate. In this case, it could be used to prescribe requirements that are more stringent than existing regulations. This could pose a trade barrier to organizations located in countries where ISO 14000 is not required by law.

A related concern is that governments will use ISO 14000 to determine legal requirements and the government's enforcement responses and to calculate criminal penalties. A key principle of TC 207's work is that international standards should not be used to create or determine legal requirements.

Doesn't Actually Lead to Better Environmental Performance

Remember that the ISO 14000 standard is a process, not a performance standard. The expectation, however, is that better management will lead to better performance. If companies achieve ISO 14000 certificates without demonstrating results, stakeholders who expect ISO registration to be a decisive indicator of environmental progress may lose confidence in the process.

Third-Party Registration Issues

Finally, there are concerns about the third-party registration process and the overall system for assessing conformity to the standards. Some of the key issues include:

- Consistent interpretation of the standards.
- The role of the self-declaration versus third-party registration for ISO 14000 implementation.
- Accreditation of the registrars (certification bodies).
- Competence of ISO 14000 auditors.
- Recognition of ISO 14000 registration certificates worldwide.

Despite these caveats, interest in ISO 14000 is increasing. The standardization process itself is an indication. Twenty-two country delegations participated in the first meeting of TC 207 in 1993. This number had grown to 47 by the June 1995 meeting.

The ISO 14000 standards are expected to generate as much, if not more, interest than did ISO 9000. One key reason is a new paradigm shift in environmental management. This the subject of the next chapter.

NOTES

1. US regulations contain hundreds of standards from a variety of sources: local, national, regional, and global. Government policy favors the use of international standards to promote trade and ease technical trade barriers. In 1993, the Office of Management and Budget (OMB) issued a revised policy statement, OMB Circular A-119, "Federal Participation in the Development and Use of Voluntary Standards." A-119 provides federal agencies with guidance on the use of private standards and participation in voluntary standards bodies. Section 7a(2) of the circular states that "International standards should be considered in procurement and regulatory applications in the interests of promoting trade and implementing the provisions of the Agreement on Technical Barriers to Trade and the Agreement on Government Procurement."

2. Colombia, for example, plans to give preference in contracts to companies that comply with ISO 14000. (Reported in "Colombia, Chile, Argentina Prepare for ISO 14001," *International Environmental Systems Update,* July 1995, p. 1.)

3. Executive Order 12873—Federal Acquisition, Recycling and Waste Prevention, October 20, 1993. Published in the Federal Register, October 22, 1993.

4. If the EPA makes some use of ISO 14000, would registration be the only route companies could follow? On the one hand, independent third-party audits can provide the confidence that the marketplace and governments require. On the other hand, registration requires resources that many companies might not have. According to Mary McKiel, Director of the EPA's Standards Network, the EPA wants to have confidence that a company has properly implemented ISO 14000 but doesn't want to disadvantage those companies that, for whatever reason, prefer self-declaration as the means of demonstrating conformance. One possible approach for acceptance of self-declaration would be to set clear criteria and for the EPA to play an active role in developing certification/registration criteria for any proposed national accreditation system.

Chapter Two

Environmental Management— The New Paradigm

This chapter sets the context for the development of ISO 14000. If it's true that "the past is prologue," then a short trip through the history of environmental management will lay the groundwork for understanding why ISO 14000? And why now?

DEVELOPMENT OF ENVIRONMENTAL MANAGEMENT

Environmental management as a discipline is perhaps a couple of decades old. Before the development of extensive environmental regulation, environmental issues were dealt with not by specialized environmental managers but by engineers and technical people with diverse backgrounds and ranges of responsibilities. Legal requirements in the environmental area were limited. Regulations related to obtaining permits and performing routine monitoring were relatively narrow in scope.[1]

Growth of Environmental Regulation

Starting in the late 1960s and early 1970s, however, things began to change. Among other nations, the United States began to erect a complex command and control regulatory framework that today fills over 20,000 pages of the *Federal Register,* not including regulations at the state and local level. Almost every step in the production process is associated with regulation, from the purchase of raw materials to the use and disposal of hazardous materials.

Companies responded in the early 1970s by creating positions for environmental managers and developing some kind of compliance assurance program, especially companies in industries associated with serious potential health, safety, and environmental problems. These programs often included environmental auditing programs to ensure compliance and demonstrate good will to the public, investors, and others.

The focus of early environmental management was on regulatory compliance. Regulations usually relied on end-of-pipe pollution control and followed the single-media focus of the major federal statutes. Key legislation in the 1970s and 1980s included the Clean Air Act (1970), the Clean Water Act (1972), the Resource Conservation and Recovery Act (1976), the Toxic Substance Control Act (1978), the Comprehensive Environmental Response, Compensation and Liability Act (1980), and the Emergency Planning and Community Right-to-Know Act (1986). The regulations generated by the EPA were complex and overlapping; state and local requirements often created another layer.

Businesses tended to focus on the requirements of each regulation, without much time or thought given to integrating their compliance procedures into a system. Environmental managers were often crisis managers, not proactive planners. Many were aware that compliance problems could often be traced back to system problems such as inadequate training, lack of responsibility at the right level, inadequate data, and other such causes, but few managers implemented changes on a system level. Nor were other functions of the business—for example, design, engineering, and manufacturing—involved in or responsible for environmental matters that affected them.

In short, environmental management has been, and too often still remains, reactive, fragmentary, and focused on putting out fires rather than preventing them from occurring in the first place. For several reasons, environmental management is now evolving into a more systematic approach.

Increasing Cost of Environmental Protection

One reason that environmental management is becoming more system-oriented is the overall cost of environmental protection. There are compliance and liability costs associated with environmental problems and costs associated with regulatory penalties and criminal sanctions.

For many companies, compliance costs have been viewed as simply the cost of doing business. As regulations grew more complex, numerous, and pervasive, however, the cost of compliance rose. The EPA predicts that the cost of one aspect of environmental protection—pollution control—is likely to double by the year 2000.[2] Environmental costs are also increasing as a percentage of company revenues. US corporations today spend about 2 percent of their sales revenues on environmental management; an estimated 20 percent of corporate capital investments are directed to environmental projects.[3] Accordingly businesses have begun to look for more cost-effective ways to deal with compliance issues.

In recent years, environmental regulations have also increased the threat of significant legal and financial liabilities. Legislation such as Superfund in the United States has enlarged corporate liability for past environmental problems. Regulatory and court decisions have broadened the liability of company boards for environmental mismanagement. This has caused more companies to take a serious look at compliance issues in order to reduce exposure.

Scrutiny from Financial Institutions

Investor and financial pressure is providing an impetus toward better management. Lenders have become more sensitized to environmental issues and are taking such issues into consideration when making loans. Increasingly, lenders are asking for verification that plants under construction or new processes will not create environmental problems that would lower their value as investments.

Single-Media to Multi-Media Regulation

Starting in the mid to late-1980s, the regulatory system in the United States began to look past end-of-pipe approaches to preventive approaches. The Federal Pollution Prevention Act of 1990 encouraged pollution prevention. Approaches have been proposed to reduce cross-media shifts (i.e., eliminating an air pollution problem only to shift the burden to water pollution). The EPA has begun to move toward a multi media approach to regulation, with strategies that address compliance across media boundaries within industry sectors.

Command and Control to Marketplace Incentives

The traditional prescriptive command and control approach to regulation is being broadened to include market incentives such as incentives taxes, emissions trading, pollution charges, carbon taxes on fuel use, and other such mechanisms.

Environment Goes Global

On a global scale, evidence suggests that environmental problems have become more widespread, and the public has become more concerned about potential problems such as global warming and stratospheric ozone depletion. Major accidents such as Bhopal, India, and the Exxon *Valdez* focused attention on the environmental impacts of industry and on the responsibility of industry to become better stewards of the environment.

Sustainable Development

While industrial activity places more burdens on the environment, the easier availability of technology, financial resources, and raw materials fuels global industry by opening new markets for nearly all companies regardless of size, location, or product. Demands for the benefits of modern industry, such as a higher standard of living and more consumer goods, are increasing in step with increasing population growth.

The challenges presented by this global context has spawned the notion of sustainable development. This concept was coined by the 1987 Brundtland Commission report, "Our Common Future." The report was the product of the United Nations World Commission on Environment and Development. It referred to sustainable development as an approach that uses the earth's resources in a way that does not compromise the ability of future generations to meet their needs. In short, it means balancing economic growth with environmental protection. This can involve implementing pollution prevention, reducing the use of toxic and waste substances, and slowing the depletion of nonrenewable resources.

The idea of sustainable development emerged in a broader sense as a result of agreements entered into at the UN Conference on the Environment in Rio de Janiero in 1992. It has become the foundation on which governments and corporations will build their environmental policies for the 21st century. The international business community has adopted the principles of sustainable development in the form of the Business Charter for Sustainable Development. The 16 proposals and requirements referred to in this document include basic elements of environmental management systems.

All of these developments have put pressure on companies to better manage their environmental responsibilities. Traditionally, business success and environmental protection have been viewed as contradictory. The cost of environmental compliance has been viewed by many companies as an impediment to competitiveness. Thus, the move by some companies to set up shop in countries with more lax requirements—the so-called race to the bottom.

In many nations, however, the paradigm is changing so that free trade and environmental protection can go hand-in-hand in pursuit of sustainable development. The challenge of the next few decades is to test this paradigm—to prove that increased economic activity can coexist with environmental protection. ISO 14000 may well play a pivotal role in meeting this challenge.

A NEW PARADIGM FOR ENVIRONMENTAL MANAGEMENT

Proactive companies are taking the lead in establishing a new paradigm for environmental management, changing it from an add-on function to one that is integral to a business's strategic planning and operations. EMS is becoming less compliance-driven and more strategy-driven. A good analogy is the quality field. Quality guru Edward Deming said that quality can't rely only on inspection at the end of the manufacturing process; it must be built into every aspect of the business, from design through manufacturing, sales, and servicing.

Similarly, environmental protection can no longer depend only on end-of-pipe controls, which are often inefficient and inadequate. Pollution prevention and other environmental issues must be addressed throughout all aspects of the design, manufacturing and distribution process.

Using a life cycle approach, R&D decisions are now emerging as standard operating procedures that take into account the use of raw materials, methods of manufacture, and the ultimate recyclability and disposability of a product.

Environment as Everyone's Responsibility

Following the quality analogy, responsibility for environmental protection is moving beyond the environmental department to all employees whose tasks have environmental aspects. Top management is also taking direct responsibility. According to a 1992 survey of Fortune 500 companies by the Investor Responsibility Research Center, almost half of the 201 respondents now have board level committees responsible for environmental affairs.

A recent Price Waterhouse survey, "Progress on the Environmental Challenge," offers more evidence of corporate responsibility: More than 40 percent of the 445 companies responding to the survey said they had elevated oversight of environmental compliance to the board level. This was almost three times that of a 1990 survey. Sixty-three percent of companies surveyed now have formal policies to account for environmental cleanup costs. Seventy-three percent of companies are conducting environmental audits, up from 40 percent in 1992. Seventeen percent of firms with significant environmental liabilities and 8 percent of those without now issue environmental annual reports. And 38 percent factor environmental performance into incentive compensation for executives and senior management.

Business Costs to Business Opportunities

Rather than viewing environmental compliance as a financial liability, increasingly businesses are recognizing competitive opportunities in pollution prevention, clean technologies, and environmentally responsible products. On a basic level, pollution prevention saves money by reducing the costs of waste disposal, raw material purchases, and energy.

Increasingly, environmental managers are discovering what has been demonstrated in the quality arena: High quality does not necessarily mean high cost, at least not in the long run. Management practices that preserve the environment can also improve the bottom line. A recent World Resources Institute study, using data derived from 10,000 factories, found that facilities with good environmental records do not sacrifice profit compared with other companies.[4]

Partly, businesses are responding to global pressure to reduce inefficiencies. They are harnessing environmental management in the service of operating efficiency. There's also pressure to achieve product differentiation. Two traditional ways are to build higher quality products and to offer better service. Another way is to design "greener" products.

THE PROLIFERATION OF ENVIRONMENTAL STANDARDS

In summary, more companies are developing EMS programs that are geared to avert compliance problems, improve operating efficiencies, and gain competitive advantage. As mentioned in Chapter 1, many of these

EMS programs have been codified in voluntary standards, industry guidelines, or other initiatives.[5] Several nations have developed national standards for environmental management systems, such as the United Kingdom's BS 7750. Then there are regional initiatives such as the European Union's Eco-Management and Audit Scheme regulation (EMAS). And over two dozen nations have developed environmental labeling (ecolabeling) programs.

Although there is much commonality among these efforts, the proliferation of differing standards worldwide for environmental management systems, environmental auditing, labeling, and other environmental processes can increase the cost of doing business and complicate international trade. Thus, there is a need to harmonize these activities by developing a single, global set of standards for environmental management systems and tools.

Enter the International Organization for Standardization (ISO) and the development of ISO 14000.

NOTES

1. See generally Frank Friedman, *Practical Guide to Environmental Management,* 6th ed. (Washington, D.C.: Environmental Law Institute, 1995).

2. U.S. Environmental Protection Agency, EPA Fact Sheet: *Environmental Investments, The Cost of a Clean Environment* (Washington, D.C.: Government Printing Office, December, 1990).

3. Ibid.

4. The study is called *Jobs, Competitiveness and Environmental Regulation.* Quoted in *Environmental Managers Compliance Advisor,* April 17, 1995, p. 2.

5. Many other voluntary initiatives, codes of practice, and standards have proliferated worldwide. One is the Environmental Self Assessment Program (ESAP), sponsored by the Global Environmental Managment Initiative, a group of 21 US corporations. ESAP emerged as a way to apply the ICC's 16 principles of sustainable development to business operations. Another such effort is the Coalition for Environmentally Responsible Economies (CERES) Principles. This effort was partly an outgrowth of the 1989 *Valdez* oil spill. CERES represents socially concerned investors who control several hundred billion dollars of investment capital.

Chapter Three

The Development of ISO 14000

Before we discuss ISO, it's important to define the role of international standards. What are they and why do we need them? For one thing, international standards allow a person to buy a Japanese video camera in the United States, use videotapes made in Europe, and play the tapes on VCRs in Brazil. Standardization allowed the authors of this book to use an ATM card in Europe and credit their accounts in the United States.

The International Organization for Standardization (ISO) defines a standard as a documented agreement containing technical specifications or other precise criteria to be used consistently as a rule, guideline, or definition of characteristics, to ensure that materials, products, processes, and services are fit for their purpose. Ideally, standards are designed to facilitate international trade by increasing the reliability and effectiveness of goods and services.

WHAT IS ISO?

Based in Geneva, Switzerland, ISO is a specialized international organization whose members are the national standards bodies of 111 countries. ISO was founded in 1946 to develop manufacturing, trade, and communication standards. Participation in ISO standards development varies by country. Some countries are represented by governmental or quasi-governmental bodies. The American National Standards Institute (ANSI) is the United States member body to ISO. The goals of ISO standards are to facilitate the efficient exchange of goods and services. All standards developed by ISO are voluntary; however, countries often adopt ISO standards and make them mandatory.

ISO is structured into approximately 180 technical committees (TCs), each of which specializes in drafting standards in a particular area. ISO develops standards in all industries except those related to electrical and electronic engineering. Standards in these areas are developed by the Geneva-based International Electrotechnical Commission (IEC), which has more than 40 member countries.

Member nations form technical advisory groups (TAGs) that provide input to the technical committees as part of the standards development process. ISO receives input from government, industry, and other interested parties before promulgating a standard. After a draft standard is voted on by all member countries, it is published as an international standard. Each nation can then adopt a version of the standard as its national standard.

The ISO Standards Process

ISO follows a few key principles in its standards development process. These include:

Consensus: The views of all interests are taken into account: manufacturers, vendors and users, consumer groups, testing laboratories, governments, engineering professions, and research organizations.

Industry-wide: The goal is to draft standards that satisfy industries and customers worldwide.

Voluntary: International standardization is market-driven and therefore based on voluntary involvement of all interests in the marketplace.

Developing a standard. International standards are developed by ISO technical committees (TC) through a five-step process:

1. Proposal stage.
2. Preparatory stage.
3. Committee stage.
4. Approval stage.
5. Publication stage.

The proposal stage confirms the need for a new standard. A new work item (NWI) proposal is submitted for vote by the members of the relevant TC or subcommittee (SC). The proposal is accepted if a majority of the

(Continued)

(Continued)

participating (P) members of the TC/SC vote in favor and at least five P members declare their commitment to participate actively in the project.

During the preparatory stage, working groups of experts develop working drafts (WD) of the proposed standard. When the working groups are satisfied that the WD is ready to become a standard, it is forwarded to the subcommittee and advanced to the committee draft (CD) stage.

The CD is registered by ISO's Central Secretariat and is distributed for voting and comments by the P members of the TC/SC. Successive committee drafts may be considered until consensus is reached on the content of the CD. It then advances to the Draft International Standard (DIS) stage.

During the approval stage, the DIS is circulated to all ISO member bodies for voting and comment within a period of six months. It is approved as an International Standard (IS) if a two-thirds majority of the P members of the TC/SC are in favor and not more than one-quarter of the total number of votes cast are negative. If the vote is negative, the DIS is returned to the TC for revision.

The final stage is publication. If the standard is approved, a final text is prepared, incorporating comments submitted during the DIS vote. The final text is sent to the ISO Central Secretariat, which publishes the International Standard.

From products to processes

For most of its history, ISO focused on product technical standards. In 1979, however, it took a sharp turn into the area of management standards. In 1979, ISO formed Technical Committee 176 (ISO TC 176) to develop global standards for quality management and quality assurance systems. The intent was to harmonize different and conflicting requirements for quality systems. The work of TC 176 culminated in 1987 with the publication of the ISO 9000 quality standards. Since ISO 9000 is largely the forerunner of ISO 14000, it's instructive to describe the basic content and rationale of the ISO 9000 series.

ISO 9000

The ISO 9000 series are generic standards for quality management and quality assurance. The basic rationale of ISO 9000 is that consistently meeting specifications for quality products and services depends partly on implementing and maintaining a systematic quality system. An effective system helps to ensure consistent results and provide confidence to customers.

Although the ultimate purpose of the ISO 9000 standards is to improve products or services, the standards do not specifically apply to products or services themselves but to the processes and systems that produce those products or services.

The ISO 9000 series standards describe the basic elements of a quality management system and provide guidance for implementing the quality system. The standards focus on basic management elements such as developing policies for quality, putting a system in place to achieve objectives, measuring and monitoring progress, reviewing the system, and making improvements. The ISO 9000 standards are used to determine whether these important elements are in place; the standards do not tell a company how it must run its business.

The ISO 9000 series covers a broad scope of quality system elements— they are flexible and relatively uncomplicated. Basically, the standards require a company to document what it does, do what it documents, review the process, and change it when necessary.

A company that has achieved ISO 9000 registration can attest that it has a documented quality system that is fully deployed and consistently followed. The standards in the series that are used for registration purposes include ISO 9001, ISO 9002, and ISO 9003. ISO 9001 is the most comprehensive and covers all elements, from design and development, through production, installation, and servicing. Other standards, such as ISO 9000 and ISO 9004, provide guidance for using the standards and for implementing their elements internally.

The ISO 9000 standards apply to all types of companies, large and small, in both manufacturing or services. The series has been adopted by over 90 countries. More than 70,000 company facilities worldwide have achieved registration to one of the three standards in the series: ISO 9001, ISO 9002, or ISO 9003.

Reasons for Registration

For some companies, registration to ISO 9000 is a legal requirement to enter regulated markets. This is the case for industry sectors such as medical devices in the European Union. In other cases, registration has also become a precondition to placing a contractual purchase order.

Governments are implementing ISO 9000, incorporating ISO 9000 requirements into their regulatory structure, or evaluating its potential to help meet regulatory goals. Agencies involved in ISO 9000 activities in the United States include the Food and Drug Administration, Department of Defense, the Federal Aviation Administration, and others.

The primary driver for ISO 9000 adoption, however, has become marketplace pressure. Compliance with ISO 9000 standards via a third-party registration process has become a de facto condition for doing business in several industry sectors. Companies have implemented ISO 9000 to maintain market share, keep up with, or get ahead of their competition.

In addition, ISO 9000–registered companies have realized internal benefits: better operating efficiency, higher quality, reduced cost, and greater productivity. The basic requirements of ISO 9000 are described in Table 3–1.

TABLE 3–1
ISO 9001 Requirements

The basic requirements of ISO 9001 are contained in 20 clauses. The following are the clauses contained in *ANSI/ASQC Q9001—1994, Quality Systems-Model for Quality Assurance in Design, Development, Production, Installation and Servicing.*

1 Scope	4.10 Inspection and testing
2 Normative reference	4.11 Control of inspection, measuring,
3 Definitions	and test equipment
4 Quality-system requirements	4.12 Inspection and test status
4.1 Management responsibility	4.13 Control of nonconforming product
4.2 Quality system	
4.3 Contract review	4.14 Corrective and preventive action
4.4 Design control	4.15 Handling, storage, packaging, preservation, and delivery
4.5 Document and data control	4.16 Control of quality records
4.6 Purchasing	4.17 Internal quality audits
4.7 Control of customer-supplied product	4.18 Training
	4.19 Servicing
4.8 Product identification and traceability	4.20 Statistical techniques
4.9 Process control	

FORMATION OF SAGE

Partly in response to the acceptance of the ISO 9000 quality management and quality assurance standard and partly in response to the proliferation of various environmental standards worldwide, ISO began to look at the environmental management field. In 1991, ISO formed the Strategic Action Group on the Environment (SAGE) to make recommendations regarding international environmental standards. SAGE was asked to investigate whether an international environmental standard could achieve the following goals:

- Promote a common approach to environmental management.
- Enhance an organization's ability to attain and measure improvements in environmental performance.
- Facilitate trade and remove trade barriers.

The members of SAGE debated the relationship between quality management and environmental management standards. Although many management elements are common to both (e.g., setting policies, defining objectives and targets, measuring, and monitoring), they concluded that the knowledge required for environmental management was distinct enough from that of quality to warrant a separate ISO technical committee and a separate standards development process. Thus, in 1992, SAGE recommended the formation of an ISO Technical Committee (TC) dedicated to developing a uniform international EMS standard.

That committee, ISO TC 207, met for the first time in June 1993, at which point SAGE was disbanded. At TC 207's first meeting, some 200 delegates representing about 30 countries expressed a desire to move as rapidly as possible to develop the first standards for environmental management systems.

Makeup and Structure of TC 207

TC 207 is divided into six international subcommittees and one working group. Subcommittee members include representatives from industry, standards organizations, government, environmental organizations, and other interested groups. Each nation sets up a technical advisory group (TAG) to the international subcommittee. Thus, in the United States, the American National Standards Institute (ANSI), which is the US representative to TC

(Continued)

(Continued)

207, set up a US TAG to TC 207. And each international subcommittee has a corresponding national subcommittee known as a SubTAG. Thus, there are SubTAGs for EMS, auditing, EPE, and so on.

The primary purpose of the TAG in each nation is to develop and transmit to ISO its national position on a particular standard in the form of comments and voting ballots. The American Society for Testing and Materials (ASTM), along with the American Society for Quality Control (ASQC), administers on behalf of the American National Standards Institute (ANSI)—the US member body to ISO—the US TAG to ISO.

Adopting ISO Standards as US National Standards

ISO standards can be used as international standards or adopted as national standards, either verbatim or with modifications. In the case of ISO 14000, the United States has developed a parallel process that calls for reviewing the international version for acceptability as a US standard at the same time that it is being developed by ISO. This will speed up the process of adoption as a US standard.

Each member country of ISO must have an accredited standards committee in place to adopt international standards. In the United States, ANSI set up the Z1 Committee on Quality Management and Quality Assurance for ISO 9000 adoption. A new Z1 subcommittee has been formed to work on the ISO 14000 process. ANSI has tasked ASTM, ASQC, and NSF International to work together to publish and sponsor the American version of the ISO 14000 standards. The US TAG votes on the acceptability of the ISO standard. They have three options:

1. If the US TAG votes to approve the standard and the three standards organizations mentioned above are satisfied that the content of the standard meets the needs of the United States, it will be published verbatim as a US standard.

2. If the organizations have reservations, they can publish a version of the standard that is not exactly the same but a technical equivalent to the ISO standard.

3. If the US TAG votes negative, which is unlikely, the standards organizations are not obligated to adopt the ISO standard as a US standard. This doesn't prevent anyone from using the ISO standard in its international form. It simply means that the United States chooses not to have its own version.

SCOPE OF TC 207

The specific scope of TC 207's work is "standardization in the field of environmental management tools and systems." ISO 14000 deals with management systems and methods, not product or technical standards. The final result of TC 207's work will be a comprehensive set of standards for every aspect of environmental management. Excluded from TC 207's scope is the following:

- Test methods for pollutants. These are the responsibility of other ISO technical committees: ISO/TC 146 (Air Quality), ISO/TC 147 (Water Quality), ISO/TC 190 (Soil Quality), and ISO/TC 43 (Acoustics),
- Setting limit values regarding pollutants or effluents.
- Setting environmental performance levels.
- Standardization of products.

System, Not Performance

TC 207's scope of work excludes anything related to actual environmental performance. This point was introduced in Chapter 1. The ISO 14000 standards are process—not performance—standards. They focus on setting up a system to achieve internally set policies, objectives, and targets. The standards require that such policies include elements such as compliance with laws and regulations and the prevention of pollution. But the standards do not dictate how the organization will achieve these goals, nor will they prescribe the type or level of performance required.

Regulations often prescribe not only performance goals but the technology with which to achieve them. In the United States, EPA regulations sometimes call for Maximum Achievable Control Technology (MACT) or Best Available Control Technology (BACT). There is rarely agreement, however, over what constitutes BACT and MACT. And industry usually resists being told which technology to use to achieve regulatory mandates. Under the European Union's EMAS regulation, companies are to include Economically Viable and Achievable Best Available Technology (EVABAT) wherever possible. Thus, EMAS has performance aspects.

In short, the ISO 14000 series, like ISO 9000, focus on the processes necessary to achieve results, not the results themselves. The goal is to increase confidence among all stakeholders that an organization has a system in place that is likely to lead to better environmental performance.

Management Systems and Tools

The work of TC 207 is divided into six subcommittees and a special working group. Canada is the Secretariat of TC 207, and six other countries head the committee's six subcommittees. As shown in Figure 3–1, several of the subcommittees are further broken down into work groups, depending on the number of standards planned by each subcommittee's scope of work. TC 207 has 43 participating members and 15 observer members.

The work on the EMS standards focuses on the basic elements needed to set up an effective environmental management system. Subcommittee 1 is developing the ISO 14001 specification standard for EMS. This is the standard that will be used for third-party registration purposes. (Registration refers to an independent third-party audit of the EMS and the consequent awarding of a certificate confirming that the organization's EMS conforms to ISO 14001 requirements.)

The auditing work looks at the generic process of auditing in the environmental area. The first standards focus specifically on environmental management system auditing methods. Future standards may describe other types of environmental auditing, such as auditing initial reviews of the environmental management system and environmental site assessment audits. (The ISO auditing standards are described in Chapter 6.)

The environmental performance evaluation work focuses on ways to measure environmental performance, how to set up an environmental performance evaluation process, and how to report performance information, both internally and externally. (Environmental performance evaluation is discussed in Chapter 7.)

The labeling work addresses the full range of environmental claims made by companies. Standards are in development for harmonizing the practices of over two dozen national ecolabeling programs and the environmental claims made by manufacturers. (Labeling standards are described in Chapter 9.)

The work on life cycle assessment (LCA) is geared to providing environmental managers and LCA practitioners with an introduction to the life cycle concept and a description of life cycle methodology. (Life cycle assessment is described in Chapter 8.)

The subcommittee on terms and definitions is helping to harmonize the definitions used in the other standards and to develop a definitions standard. A high priority of TC 207 is to create a common, international language for environmental management.

36

FIGURE 3-1
ISO/TC 207 Subcommittees and Working Groups

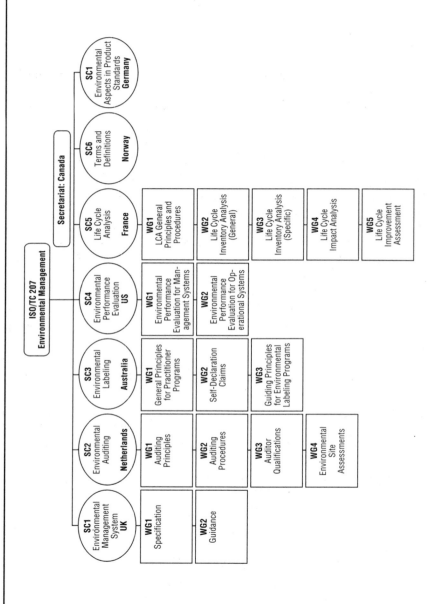

Finally, the special Working Group 1 committee is developing a standard on the environmental aspects in product standards that is designed for standards writers. (Chapter 10.) It will acquaint them with the ways in which environmental issues come into play when writing product technical standards.

The main purpose of these standards is more uniform, efficient, and effective environmental management by organizations worldwide. A list of the developing standards in the ISO 14000 family is shown in Table 3–2.

TABLE 3–2
TC 207 Subcommittees and Standards

SC1—Environmental Management Systems (EMS)

WG1—ISO/DIS 14001 Environmental management systems. Specification with guidance for use.

WG2—ISO/DIS 14004 Environmental management systems. General guidelines on principles, systems, and supporting techniques.

SC2—Environmental Auditing

WG1—ISO/DIS 14010 Guidelines for environmental auditing. General principles of environmental auditing.

WG2—ISO/DIS 14011/1 Guidelines for environmental auditing. Audit procedures—Part 1: Auditing of environmental management systems.

WG3—ISO/DIS 14012 Guidelines for environmental auditing. Qualification criteria for environmental auditors.

WG4—ISO 14015 Environmental site assessments (proposed new work item).

SC3—Environmental Labeling

WG1—ISO/CD 14024 Environmental labeling—practitioner programs. Guiding principles, practices, and certification procedures of multiple-criteria programs.

WG2—ISO/CD 14021 Environmental labeling—self-declaration environmental claims. Terms and definitions.

WG2—ISO 14022 Environmental labeling—symbols; ISO 14023 Environmental labeling—Testing and verification methodologies (in progress).

WG3—ISO/CD 14020 Goals and principles of all environmental labeling.

SC4—Environmental Performance Evaluation

WG1/WG2—ISO/CD 14031 Evaluation of the environmental performance of the management system and its relationship to the environment.

SC5—Life Cycle Assessment

WG1—ISO/CD 14040 Environmental management—life cycle assessment. General principles and guidelines.

WG2/WG3—ISO/WD 14041 Environmental management—life cycle assessment. Inventory analysis.

(Continued)

TABLE 3-2
TC 207 Subcommittees and Standards (continued)

WG4—Environmental management—life cycle assessment. Impact assessment (work in progress).
WG5—Environmental management—life cycle assessment. Improvement assessment (work in progress).
SC6—Terms and Definitions
ISO 14050—Terms and definitions (proposed working document).
WG1—Environmental Aspects in Product Standards
ISO/CD 14060—Guide for the inclusion of environmental aspects in product standards.

Conformance Versus Guidance

A key point to remember is that of the many standards in the developing ISO 14000 family, only ISO 14001—the specification for an EMS system—is designed for third-party registration purposes. *All other standards are for guidance purposes only.* Of course, an organization can also use the ISO 14001 specification standard for internal guidance only or for self-declaration purposes. It may choose not to seek third-party verification of its EMS system. The point is that if the organization chooses to seek registration, the registration audit will focus on conformity to ISO 14001 requirements.

Of the other guidance standards, there is a possibility that one of the labeling standards could form the basis for some type of third-party verification. This is the standard focusing on harmonizing criteria and procedures for the over two dozen national labeling programs worldwide. The global marketplace may see value in having these programs demonstrate, via a third-party verification process, that their procedures conform to the labeling guidelines. For now, however, this is speculative.

Stand-Alone Standards

Another central concept is that standards in the ISO 14000 family can be used as stand-alone documents. The ISO 14001 EMS specification and the ISO 14004 guidance standard describe the basic elements of an effective EMS program. An organization can use only the EMS standards if those are sufficient for its needs. Or it can implement the guidance from one of the other standards. For example, it can develop an environmental performance evaluation (EPE) process using guidance from the work of SC4. At the same time, the EPE process can be helpful to an organization that doesn't have an EMS.

The chapters in this book that describe the guidance standards will explain the possible role of each standard within the overall ISO 14000 family.

Guidance Standards Do Not Become Requirements

The fact that an organization uses the guidance standards as part of their EMS development does not imply that the elements in those guidance standards become requirements during a third-party audit. That is, if an organization seeks registration of its EMS and has implemented the guidance from other standards such as the environmental auditing or the environmental performance evaluation standards, the auditor should not make the elements from those standards mandatory in the audit.

ISO 9000, ISO 14000, and Other Management Standards

Many members of ISO have recognized that ISO's developing management standards (quality and environment, so far) share generic management elements. These include setting policies, controlling operational processes, establishing document control procedures, and so on.

A long-term proposal under consideration by TC 207 is to develop an overarching series of general management standards that contain the elements common to all management standards, with guidance documents that explain how to implement these elements in particular areas such as quality, environment, health, and safety.

ISO 9000 and ISO 14000. TC 207 and TC 176 have formed a liaison committee to work together to harmonize the ISO 9000 and ISO 14000 series. The group is studying the elements and structure of both families of standards, including the auditing standards (ISO 10011 and ISO 14010–12). The aim is to prevent incompatibilities and, if possible, to integrate the approaches and architectures used by each set of standards to make them user friendly. Those organizations that choose to implement more than one management standard, such as both ISO 9000 and ISO 14000,

(Continued)

(Continued)

have an interest in efficient implementation of both standards and, if registration to both is sought, a single integrated audit. According to its strategic plan, TC 207 supports the possible integration of management standards such as ISO 9000 and ISO 14000, but not at the expense of neglecting the unique requirements of environmental management.

Occupational health and safety. The next possible area of development for management standards may be occupational health and safety. The United Kingdom has developed a guidance standard entitled *BS 8750 Guide to Occupational Health and Safety Management.* Other countries are also developing OH&S standards. Neither TC 207 nor TC 176 supports any plan to set up separate technical committees to address these topics and view them as falling within their existing scope. TC 176 members stress the close relationship between product quality and safety and health management. TC 207, in turn, stresses the close link between health and safety and the environment. There will be a conference in late 1995 or early 1996 to discuss the merits of an OH&S standard. The ISO Technical Management Board will then determine whether an OH&S standard is necessary and which technical committee (TC 176, TC 207, or a new committee) will develop it.

Sector-Specific Guidelines

Sector-specific *guidelines* offer information and practical advice on the interpretation and application of generic standards such as ISO 14000 in a specific industry. Such guidelines are often developed by industry associations. Industries can also develop sector-specific *supplemental requirements* by adopting the generic international specification standard but supplementing it with additional requirements relevant to their industry. This strategy was followed by the big three US automakers in their development of the QS-9000 standards. QS 9000 incorporates all the requirements of the ISO 9001 specification standard and adds additional requirements germane to the auto industry.

Sector-specific *guidance standards,* however, are different. They are often proposed as sector-specific variations to the primary specification standard, geared to a particular industry. ISO generally supports the former options (industry guidelines, supplementary requirements) when developed

(Continued)

(Continued)

by industry groups, but does not support the latter. According to its strategic plan, TC 207 views the proliferation of such standards as potentially undermining the basic concept of an international consensus standard.

Proposed forest products standard. In May 1995, Standards Council of Canada and Standards Australia proposed a new work item (NWI) for a guidance standard entitled *Guide to Application of ISO 14001 in the Forestry Sector for Sustainable Forest Management.* The proposed standard would describe how to implement the requirements of ISO 14001 and the principles of sustainable forest management in the forestry sector. It would be based on principles and criteria of sustainable forest management that are being developed by multilateral, national, public, and private-sectors organizations, including the United Nation's Commission on Sustainable Development. The proposal was opposed by many groups, including environmental groups who generally believe that the ISO 14000 standards, while useful as management standards, do not go far enough to ensure better forestry management performance. It was also opposed by industry groups such as the American Forest and Paper Association, who believe that an international standard for sustainable forestry is not practical, since flexibility is required to manage widely divergent forestry challenges in different countries.

In the face of such opposition and TC 207's stated policy to discourage sector-specific guidance standards, the proposal was withdrawn as an NWI at the June 1995 TC 207 meeting. It was presented, instead, as a discussion document for the purpose of opening a dialogue with all stakeholders interested in advancing sustainable forestry principles.

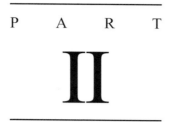

ENVIRONMENTAL MANAGEMENT
Organization Evaluation

Internal Organization for Standardization
Technical Committee 207

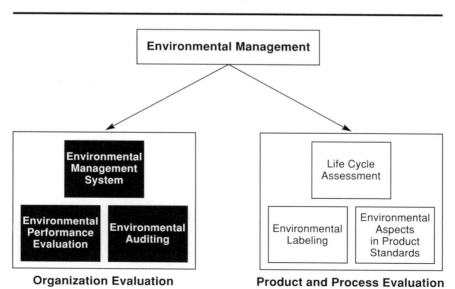

Chapter Four

The Environmental Management System Standards

The development of useful and practical standards for the environmental management system is the foundation of TC 207's work. Subcommittee 1 is developing the specification standard for EMS, ISO 14001, and a guidance standard for environmental management, ISO 14004. The ISO 14001 standard describes the basic requirements of an environmental management system. It is the standard that companies will implement and the standard to which they will either self-declare conformance or seek third-party registration. ISO 14004 is a guidance standard that provides companies with valuable information about implementing an EMS. This chapter introduces the two standards and summarizes the requirements of ISO 14001.

Both ISO 14004 and ISO 14001 advanced to Draft International Standard status in July 1995 and have been submitted to all members of TC 207 for voting purposes. They could be published as International Standards by mid-1996.

ISO 14004 VERSUS ISO 14001

It's critical to understand the difference between ISO 14004 and ISO 14001. ISO 14001 is the specification standard. The principal use of ISO 14001 is anticipated to be third-party registration, although it can be used internally, for self-declaration purposes, and in contractual situations. The primary use, however, is likely to be third-party certification. Thus, ISO 14001 contains only those requirements that may be objectively audited against for registration purposes and/or for self-declaration purposes.

In contrast, ISO 14004 is a guidance standard. It offers useful guidance in the form of examples and descriptions related to the development and implementation of environmental management systems and principles and how to coordinate these with other management systems. Although ISO 14001 and ISO 14004 share key concepts and definitions, ISO 14004 is intended for use as a voluntary, internal management tool and not intended for use by EMS certification/registration bodies as a specification standard.[1]

The discussion in this chapter will focus on the requirements described in ISO 14001. Where relevant, however, it will include information from the informative annex to ISO 14001, Annex A (which is not part of the requirements of the specification), and from the ISO 14004 guidance standard.

ISO 14001—BASIC TERMS AND DEFINITIONS

A key goal of the entire ISO 14000 process is to create a common international language for environmental management. To that end, definitions are critical and have been the subject of lengthy debate in the ISO 14000 development process.

Organization

Organization is referred to in Clause 3.12 of ISO 14001 as "a company, corporation, operation, firm, enterprise, institution, parts or combinations thereof, whether incorporated or not, public or private that has its own function and administration." If a company is registering to ISO 14001, the actual scope of the registration may apply to a site, a plant, a portion of a site, or several sites that share the same environmental management system. A note to the definition adds the clarification that "for bodies or establishments with more than one operating unit, a single operating unit may be defined as an organization." It's up to the organization, working with the registrar, to define the precise scope of the EMS and the products, processes, or services to which it applies.

Environment

The environment is defined in ISO 14001 as the surroundings in which an organization operates, including "air, water, land, natural resources, flora, fauna, humans and their interrelation." The environment extends from within the organization to the global system.

From a practical point of view, the environment that concerns a company would be the surroundings in which an organization's activities, products, and service have a significant environmental impact and over which the organization can exercise some reasonable control or influence. This influence and control can extend from local, through regional, and even to global conditions, depending on the nature of the organization.

Environmental Aspect

An environmental aspect is defined in ISO 14001 as an "element of an organization's activities, products and/or services which can interact with the environment." A note to the definition defines a significant environmental aspect as "an environmental aspect which has or can have a significant environmental impact." It's up to the organization to identify the environmental aspects of its products, processes, and services when setting up an EMS.

Environmental Impact

An environmental impact is "any change to the environment, whether adverse or beneficial, wholly or partially resulting from an organization's activities, products and/or services." The environmental aspects of an organization's activities create environmental impacts.

Environmental Management System

An environmental management system is "that part of the overall management system which includes organizational structure, planning activities, responsibilities, practices, procedures, processes and resources for developing, implementing, achieving, reviewing and maintaining the environmental policy."

Environmental Management System Audit

This is a "systematic and documented verification process to objectively obtain and evaluate evidence to determine whether an organization's environmental management system conforms to the environmental management system audit criteria" that are set by the organization itself. The definition also adds that the results of the EMS audit process must be communicated to management.

Environmental Performance

Environmental performance refers to "measurable results of the environmental management system, related to an organization's control of the environmental aspects based on its environmental policy, objectives and targets."[2]

Continual Improvement

Continual improvement refers to the "process of enhancing the environmental management system to achieve improvements in overall environmental performance in line with the organization's policy." A note adds that "the process need not take place in all areas of activity simultaneously."

INTRODUCTION TO ISO 14001

The Introduction to ISO 14001 points out that organizations of all kinds want to achieve and demonstrate effective environmental performance. One way to do this is to control the environmental impacts of their activities, products, and/or services. This can occur through environmental audits or reviews. However, while these are useful tools, they are not sufficient or comprehensive. To ensure that the organization meets its goals, audits should be part of a larger framework, "a structured management system that is integrated with overall management activity." Therefore, the basic purpose of ISO 14001 is to provide organizations with the basic requirements of an effective EMS system.

Applicability

The standard is applicable to all types and sizes of organizations. It's meant to accommodate diverse geographical, cultural, and social conditions and to be successfully applied everywhere.[3]

A critical point mentioned earlier is that the standard does not establish "absolute requirements for environmental performance beyond commitment, in the policy, to compliance with applicable legislation and regulations and to continual improvement." The implication is that two organizations that perform similar activities and achieve different environmental performance can both conform to ISO 14001.

The EMS described in ISO 14001 applies to those environmental aspects which the organization can control and over which it can be expected to have an influence. It does not itself state specific environmental performance criteria.

An ISO 14001 registration will not guarantee that a particular facility has achieved the best possible environmental performance, only that it has the basic elements of an EMS in place. The continual improvement mentioned in the standard refers to continual improvement of the management system, not of environmental performance directly.

Annex A to ISO 14001 emphasizes that the basic purpose of an EMS is to provide an organization with a structured process and a framework with which to achieve and systematically control the level of environmental performance it sets for itself. The actual level of performance depends on economic, regulatory, and other circumstances.

The standard notes that its adoption "will not in itself guarantee optimal environmental outcomes." Of course, the basic theme is that over the long run, organizations with an effective EMS will improve their performance. The Introduction to ISO 14001 states that in order to achieve its objectives, the environmental management system "should encourage organizations to consider implementation of best available technology where appropriate and where economically viable." The use of best available technology, however, is not a requirement of ISO 14001.

Does Not Include Health and Safety

The standard does not address requirements for occupational health and safety management and such requirements will not be audited. On the other hand, the standard doesn't prevent organizations from incorporating health and safety issues into their EMS programs. Again, many organizations may adapt an EMS from existing environmental, health, and safety programs.

No Need to Reinvent the Wheel

The Introduction to ISO 14001 also points out that ISO 14001 shares many common management principles with ISO 9000. Thus, organizations can adapt an existing ISO 9000 system to use as a basis for an EMS. The point is that a company need not reinvent the wheel by establishing ISO 14001 elements that are independent of existing management systems. Environmental management is an integral part of an organization's overall management system, and its elements should be coordinated with existing efforts in other areas.

Scope

When an organization registers to ISO 14001 or self-declares compliance, it declares that a specific EMS complies with the standard. The EMS can cover the entire organization, a specific facility or operating unit, or several facilities. It's up to the organization to decide the level of detail and complexity of the EMS and to which activities, processes, and products it applies.

ISO 14001 REQUIREMENTS

The following is an explanation of the ISO 14001 requirements (see Table 4–1). *Minimal interpretation of the standard is offered, since it is technically in draft form. Whenever an interpretation is offered, it will be clearly indicated as such.*

The EMS requirements are contained in Section 4 of ISO 14001. The most basic requirement, in Clause 4.0, is to establish and maintain an EMS that includes all requirements described in the standard. The basic model for an EMS is described in the ISO 14004 guidance document as a five-step process:

Commitment and policy. In this phase, the organization defines an environmental policy and ensures commitment to it.

Planning. The organization formulates a plan to fulfill the policy.

Implementation. The organization puts the plan into action by providing resources and support mechanisms.

Measurement and evaluation. The organization measures, monitors, and evaluates its environmental performance against its objectives and targets.

Review and improvement. The organization reviews and continually improves the EMS to achieve improvements in overall environmental performance.

TABLE 4-1
ISO/DIS 14001 Environmental Management Systems—Specification with Guidance for Use

0	Introduction	4.3.3	Communication
1	Scope	4.3.4	Environmental management system documentation
2	References		
3	Definitions	4.3.5	Document control
4	Environmental management system requirements	4.3.6	Operational control
		4.3.7	Emergency preparedness and response
4.0	General		
4.1	Environmental policy	4.4	Checking and corrective action
4.2	Planning	4.4.1	Monitoring and measurement
4.2.1	Environmental aspects	4.4.2	Nonconformance and corrective and preventive action
4.2.2	Legal and other requirements		
4.2.3	Objectives and targets	4.4.3	Records
4.2.4	Environmental management programs	4.4.4	Environmental management system audit
4.3	Implementation and operation	4.5	Management review
4.3.1	Structure and responsibility	Annex A (Informative) Guidance on the use of the specification	
4.3.2	Training, awareness, and competence	Annex B Bibliography	

Environmental Policy

According to Clause 4.1, the first step in designing an EMS is to define an environmental policy and ensure commitment to it. ISO 14001 defines an environmental policy as a statement "by the organization of its intentions and principles in relation to its overall environmental performance." The environmental policy gives an overall sense of the organization's direction and commitment to the environment and provides a framework for setting goals and objectives.

Familiar policy statements include phrases such as:

"Company X is committed to protecting the environment and the health and safety of all its employees and customers."

"Company X's plants and products comply with all applicable governmental standards as well as Company X's internal standards and policies."

"Company X is dedicated to implementing methods and strategies for preventing pollution, reducing waste, and conserving resources."

Many organizations already have environmental policies. For those that do not, the most obvious areas to focus on would be regulatory compliance or areas of potential environmental liability. The policy can refer to guiding environmental principles developed by industry associations, government, and public interest groups. It can consider the organization's mission, core values, the requirements of interested parties, and specific local or regional conditions. It will respond to financial and business requirements. The policy is usually set organizationwide by the owners, board of directors, or other governing body, and top management is responsible for formulating, implementing, and modifying the policy.

The policy should be clear, be reviewed periodically, and be revised to reflect changing conditions.

The ISO 14004 guidance standard advises organizations that haven't developed a policy to begin where they can achieve obvious benefits, for example, by focusing on regulatory compliance, identifying and limiting sources of liability, or identifying more efficient ways to use materials and energy.

Key Requirements of the Policy

Whatever the specific contents of an organization's policy, ISO 14001 requires that it:

- Be appropriate to the nature, scale, and environmental impacts of the organization's activities, products, and services.
- Include a commitment to continual improvement.
- Include a commitment to prevention of pollution.
- Include a commitment to comply with relevant legislation, regulations, and other requirements to which the organization subscribes.
- Provide a framework for setting and reviewing environmental objectives and targets.
- Be documented, implemented, maintained, and communicated to all employees.
- Be made available to the public.

Much discussion and negotiation went into developing these policy requirements. Key points to note include the following.

Commitment to compliance. First, there must be a commitment to comply with all applicable laws and regulations. ISO 14001 registration is not a substitute for but instead is complementary to compliance with national laws and regulations.

Prevention of pollution. Prevention of pollution in the context of ISO 14001 is a broad concept and is defined as the "use of processes, practices, materials or products that avoid, reduce or control pollution, which may include recycling, treatment, process changes, control mechanisms, efficient use of resources and material substitution." This broad definition offers companies and nations around the world flexibility in interpreting the kinds of pollution methods they can use to fulfill these requirements. Note that the definition does not include waste, since waste need not be pollution.

Continual improvement. Third, continual improvement, as discussed earlier, refers to continual improvement of the *management system.* Again, there is general agreement that the ultimate purpose of improving the system is to improve environmental performance in some fashion, but the standard focuses on process, not performance.[4]

Includes Internal Policies and Standards

The requirements to which the organization can declare compliance can also include internal policies, including those for health and safety, existing audit program standards, corporate emergency response policies, and other such requirements. These can be stated directly in the policy.

An effective policy statement can be general—it can and should reflect the company's mission and its core values. But it shouldn't be presented in vague, lofty statements that can't be translated into clear objectives and measurable targets.

Top Management Commitment

As with any management system, policies without top-management commitment are worthless. Top management refers not to the management of the environmental program, such as the environmental vice president, but to the top management of the organization itself. Top management communicates the environmental policies and its commitment to them to all employees. The message is that achieving the policy is everyone's responsibility. In most companies where management gets support for the policy, it's because employees are given tangible rewards for achieving environmental objectives.

PLANNING

The next major requirement in ISO 14001 is Clause 4.2 Planning. The planning phase has five basic steps:

1. Identify environmental aspects of the organization's activities, products, and services that it can control and influence.
2. Determine which are associated with significant environmental impacts.
3. Identify and maintain access to legal and all other requirements that apply to the environmental aspects of the activities, products, and services.
4. Establish objectives and targets.
5. Establish the EMS.

One point to note: ISO 14001 requires planning but not necessarily a written strategic plan. Planning is usually communicated by way of written documents; ISO 14001, however, does not explicitly require these.

Environmental Aspects

An environmental aspect is defined in Clause 3.3 as an "element of an organization's activities, products and services which can interact with the environment." A note to the definition adds that "a significant environmental aspect is an environmental aspect that has or can have a significant environmental impact."

In Clause 4.2.1, the specification standard requires the organization to establish and maintain an up-to-date procedure to identify the environmental aspects of its activities, products, and services. Does this mean all aspects? No, the standard limits these to those aspects that the organization ". . . can control and over which it can be expected to have an influence, in order to determine those which have or can have significant impacts on the environment. The organization shall ensure that these aspects are considered in setting its environmental objectives."

A company may be concerned about the environmental aspects of the actual use of its products by customers. But if it has no practical control over the environmental impacts caused by customer use, then it would not take them into consideration in its EMS. It might focus on activities it can control, such as proper handling and disposal. Similarly, a contractor or supplier may have minimal control over the environmental aspects of a product while the facility responsible for product design has much more control—for example, it can change an input material.

One way to focus on aspects is to work back from regulatory and legal requirements or legal and business exposure that affects the organization's activities. Government regulations already reflect key environmental aspects of industrial activity.

Another way, as mentioned in the ISO 14004 guidance standard, is to focus on products and services that create any change, either positive or negative, to the environment. Obvious choices would include activities that result in air emissions, water releases, contamination of land, solid waste, or any use of raw materials and other natural resources. Companies can also look at the results of any environmental risk assessments, any information, if available, about previous environmental incidents, and all existing environmental management practices.

The exercise of identifying environmental aspects encourages employees to look at environmental issues that they may not have considered previously. The analysis may involve the use of a life cycle approach to examine areas of the organization's operations that may not have been considered "environmental," such as R&D (environmental considerations of product design), purchasing (evaluating alternative raw materials), or office operations (housekeeping, recycling). There are also environmental aspects in planning for new construction projects or modifications to existing projects.

The purpose of identifying environmental aspects is to determine which have or can have significant environmental impacts. This ensures that the aspects relative to these significant impacts are reflected in the company's objectives and targets. Identifying environmental aspects is an ongoing process, and the standard requires that organizations keep the information up-to-date.

Environmental Impacts

The next step is to identify, evaluate, and prioritize the significant environmental impacts associated with the environmental aspects of the activities, products, or services. The standard emphasizes, in Clause 4.2.1, that it is aspects associated with significant impacts that "are considered in setting its environmental objectives." Impacts are defined in ISO 14001 as "any change to the environment, whether adverse or beneficial, wholly or partially resulting from an organization's activities, products and services." *Aspects are activities that interact with the environment; impacts are the change in the environment resulting from that interaction.*

According to the ISO 14004 guidance standard, the relationship between environmental aspects and impacts is that of cause and effect. The aspect is the cause, such as an air emission; the effect is the environmental impact, such as the increase in the level of the emission in the environment of the plant. The guidance standard suggests a four-step procedure for identifying aspects and impacts:

1. Select an activity or process (e.g., hazardous materials handling).

2. Identify all possible environmental aspects of the activity or process (e.g., potential accidental spills).

3. Identify potential or actual impacts associated with the aspect. (e.g., soil and/or water contamination levels).

4. Evaluate significance of impacts.

Once the environmental impacts are defined, it is necessary to determine their significance. To evaluate significance, the ISO 14004 guidance standard notes factors such as:

- The scale of the impact.
- Its severity.
- The probability of its occurrence.
- The duration of its impact.

For example, paper use at the corporate headquarters of a company is an activity with an environmental aspect—it produces waste. The impact is the amount of waste disposed. This could be reduced by recycling. But if the company has a serious toxic emissions problem, this would be considered more important than the recycling opportunity.

Annex A to ISO 14001 points out that the process of identifying environmental aspects should consider normal operating conditions as well as foreseeable emergency situations. The ISO 14004 guidance standard also indicates that business concerns play a role in evaluating the significance of impacts and the extent to which they can be controlled.

Legal and Other Requirements

In Clause 4.2.2, the ISO 14001 standard requires an organization to have some way to keep track of legal and other requirements that apply to the environmental aspects of its activities, products, and services. This includes requirements specific to the activity, such as an operating permit or license, and those related to the organization's products or services, such as specific regulations or general environmental laws.

The Annex to ISO 14001 points out that "other requirements" can include industry codes of practice, nonregulatory guidelines, and agreements with public authorities (such as consent decrees). It can also include internal requirements that the organization has developed, such as supplier and contractor requirements and pollution prevention programs.

Finally, it can include international agreements, such as environmental treaties, or international guidelines, such as the 16 principles of the International Chamber of Commerce's Business Charter for Sustainable Development.

Note that the requirement is to "have access to" requirements. The assumption is that organizations need not actually maintain all requirements on site, or at every plant, but to be able to access them when necessary by those who need the information, perhaps through an electronic computer network or similar means.

OBJECTIVES AND TARGETS

The next major step is to transform the environmental policy and those environmental aspects of the organization's activities, products, and processes that have significant environmental impacts, into specific objectives and targets. Without specific objectives, the environmental policy remains a set of vague generalities that are unlikely to make much difference. An environmental objective is defined in ISO 14001 Clause 3.3 as an "overall environmental goal, arising from the environmental policy that an organization sets itself to achieve, and which is quantified where practicable."

The primary requirement in Clause 4.2.3 of ISO 14001 is to "establish and maintain documented environmental objectives and targets at each relevant function and level within the organization." The objectives and targets can apply across the organization or be site-specific or activity-specific. The overall objectives—that is, to reduce waste—are linked to specific targets for all levels of the organization. The overall goal of the organization may be to reduce air emissions by 50 percent within two years. This may translate into specific reduction targets applicable to several plants, with each target reflecting the plant's unique circumstances and environmental conditions.

While objectives are long-term goals, targets are short-term steps along the way to meeting the objectives. They should be specific, measurable, and have specific time frames for achievement, where possible. For example:

- Objective: Reduce use of chemical solvents and substitute biodegradable cleaners.
- Target: Reduce use of chemical solvents 80 percent by 1997.

Another example could be an objective to reduce waste in the form of waste produced per quantity of finished product. Or it could be the percentage of waste recycled. The target might be to reduce waste by 10 percent by a certain time. Another objective might be to reduce release of pollutants into the environment. The target may be a reduction by 20 percent in the quantity of CO_2 emissions in 1996.

The objective may be to increase recycling. The target is a 50 percent increase in the percentage of recycled material used in packaging in 1996 or a 20 percent increase in the amount of material recycled.

Still another objective might be to increase employee training and awareness of environmental issues. One way to measure this may be the number of training hours per employee. The specific target may be to increase the number of hours by 50 percent.

As with any management process, objectives can be long term or short term. In the short term, a company may want to ensure regulatory compliance and begin to reduce waste, or look at the obvious environmental aspects that it has not been dealing with systematically. Over the long term, it may want to incorporate other issues into its objectives and targets, such as design improvements or sophisticated pollution prevention technologies.

The ISO 14004 guidance standard suggests that organizations enlist the help of those employees responsible for achieving the objectives and targets to assist in developing them and also to consider the views of interested external parties.

Environmental Performance Evaluation

When setting objectives and targets, the organization can use environmental performance indicators. These are specific measurements of performance such as:

- Waste produced per quantity of finished product.
- Percent of waste recycled.
- Specific quantities of pollutants.
- Acres of land area set aside for wildlife habitat.
- Number of regulatory violations.

These indicators can create the basis for an ongoing environmental performance evaluation (EPE) process that can provide useful input to the EMS. Subcommittee 4's EPE standard is discussed in Chapter 7.

Best Available Technology

The ISO 14001 standard does not require that organizations use best available technology where economically viable (EVABAT). This would be a prescriptive requirement that reduces the flexibility of the standard; for one thing, there may be alternative ways for the organization to achieve its objectives. The standard, in Clause 4.2.3, says only that when setting objectives and targets, the organization consider "its technological options." The Annex to ISO 14001 offers EVABAT as an option "where economically viable, cost effective and judged appropriate by the organization.[5]

Environmental Cost Accounting

The standard mentions that when establishing objectives, an organization "shall consider financial, operational, and business requirements." The Annex to ISO 14001 points out that this doesn't imply that ISO 14001 requires the use of environmental cost accounting methods to track the costs and benefits of environmental performance, such as the cost of pollution control, waste, and disposal. The organization, however, is free to use these techniques if it finds them useful.

Prevention of Pollution

ISO 14001 specifically requires organizations to set objectives and targets for prevention of pollution, consistent with the environmental policy. As noted earlier, prevention of pollution is a broad concept and can include any methods to avoid, reduce, or control pollution, such as recycling, process changes, resource efficiency, or materials substitution and so on.

ENVIRONMENTAL MANAGEMENT PROGRAM

The final step in planning is to set up and maintain an environmental management system that can achieve the company's objectives and targets. According to Clause 4.2.4, the organization must:

- Designate responsibility for achieving objectives and targets at each relevant function and level.
- Provide the means for fulfilling the objectives and targets.
- Designate a time frame within which they will be achieved.

Basically, the EMS details what must be done, by whom, how, and by when. It can be subdivided into individual processes and procedures applicable to sites or facilities within a site. The ISO 14004 guidance standard emphasizes that employees at all levels should be accountable, within the scope of their responsibilities, for environmental performance that supports the overall EMS system.

For example, an organization's policy might be to reduce pollution. One objective is to reduce chemical emissions into a body of water at a site. The target is a 20 percent reduction by the end of 1996. The action plan may be to substitute a biodegradable chemical for the toxic chemical in use. The action plan details the person(s) responsible; the human, financial, and technical resources necessary; and the proposed date of completion.

The means to fulfill the objectives refers to all necessary resources that include people, skills, technology, financial resources, and so on.

Annex A points out that the EMS usually covers planning, design, materials, production processes, marketing, and disposal stages. For new installations or significant modifications, it can include planning, design, construction, commissioning, operation, and also decommissioning. New activities may require environmental reviews.

Flexibility

The ISO 14001 standard, in Clause 4.2.4, requires the EMS program to be amended, where relevant, whenever there are new or modified developments. The EMS can be independent of or integrated into the organization's overall management system. The implication is that addressing the environmental aspects of the company's activities doesn't necessarily require a separate EMS bureaucracy. It may mean introducing environmental considerations to parts of the organization that haven't dealt with them previously, such as product design or marketing.

Nor does the standard necessarily require detailed EMS plans separate from general company planning. If an organization has minimal management systems in place, more EMS planning might be necessary than in those organizations with well-developed systems.

A key theme in ISO 14001 is aligning the EMS with other management elements, such as operational controls, resource allocation, information systems, training and development, measurement and monitoring systems, and communication and reporting programs.

One goal of the entire ISO 14000 process is to make the standards practical for small and medium-size organizations. Avoiding unnecessary bureaucracy for organizations that don't have the resources or personnel to implement the bureaucracy is one way to achieve that goal.

IMPLEMENTATION AND OPERATION

The next major step in the EMS process is to implement the program. This means getting human, physical, and financial resources in place to achieve the company's objectives and targets. In Clause 4.3, the standard focuses on the following areas:

- Structure and responsibility.
- Training, awareness, and competence.
- Communications.
- EMS documentation.
- Document control.
- Operational control.
- Emergency preparedness and response.

Structure and Responsibility

As with any management system, the ISO 14001 standard, in Clause 4.3.1, requires the organization to:

- Define, document, and clearly communicate roles, responsibilities, and authorities to implement the EMS.
- Provide human, financial, and technical resources essential to doing so.

To achieve this, top management must appoint a "specific management representative(s) who, irrespective of other responsibilities" must ensure that the program is being maintained and implemented and is responsible for reporting on the performance of the EMS to top management.

The management representative. The ISO 9000 standards for quality management also use the words "irrespective of other responsibilities." Just who is the management representative? Where does this person fall in the organizational structure?

Annex A to ISO 14001 points out that in large organizations there can be several designated representatives, while in smaller companies there may be only one. In a very small company, the owner can also be the person responsible for the EMS. To accommodate a wide range of organizations, the standard is flexible.

The representative can be the chief environmental manager or an environmental committee that includes managers from across all corporate functions. The implication is that it's up to the organization to determine where the management representative fits into the corporate hierarchy. Overseeing the EMS may be and probably should be the representative's primary, although not necessarily only, responsibility.

The ISO 14004 guidance standard emphasizes that the management representative should have sufficient authority, responsibility, and resources to make sure the EMS is implemented effectively.

Organizationwide Commitment

A key theme implied in ISO 14001 is that environmental performance isn't just the environmental manager's responsibility. Everyone in the organization has a role to play. Environmental responsibilities can extend beyond the traditional environmental areas of the organization. Managers in every area are responsible for ensuring compliance to the EMS and for assigning responsibilities to employees whose work is relevant to the environmental objectives.

Communication is critical so that all employees understand their role in environmental performance. In many organizations environmental issues have been compartmentalized or limited to just the environmental department. Other employees haven't been aware of the potential environmental aspects of their jobs.

ISO 14000 implementation invites a cultural change. For the first time, sales and marketing people may be dealing with environmental issues related to product marketing. The R&D department may start taking environmental considerations into account when developing product designs. The purchasing department may take a closer look at their supplier network and at the types of products and services they buy. Finance managers may get involved in environmental cost accounting. Just as quality evolved from being just the quality inspector's job to becoming everyone's job, environmental management requires the same shift in attitudes to ensure that environmental performance is everyone's responsibility.

Training, Awareness, and Competence

In Clause 4.3.2, ISO 14001 requires that the organization set up a procedure to identify training needs and make sure all personnel "whose work may create a significant impact upon the environment" receive appropriate training. As implied above, since the success of the EMS depends on employee commitment, it also requires extensive employee competence. The training required depends on the job. It will be more extensive and skill-based for those employees who are involved directly in key environmental activities. It can focus on training in environmental compliance for anyone whose job can affect compliance requirements.

But everyone should have basic awareness training to acquaint them with the EMS. Clause 4.3.2 requires that all employees or members of the organization must be made aware of:

- Their roles and responsibilities within the context of the EMS.
- Significant environmental impacts, actual or potential, of their work activities.
- Importance of conforming with environmental policies, procedures, and EMS requirements.

- Environmental benefits of improved personal performance.
- The consequences of violating procedures.

The ISO 14004 guidance standard points out that organizations with effective training programs:

- Identify training needs.
- Develop training plans.
- Verify that the training program conforms to regulatory and other requirements.
- Provide the training.
- Document the training.
- Improve the training program.

Contractors

The ISO 14001 standard doesn't require an organization that has contractors working on its behalf to monitor the training of the contractors' employees. But Annex A suggests that the organization should require contractors to "demonstrate that their employees have the requisite training." This involves the contractor's offering some evidence of this training to the organization.

Communications

The standard recognizes the need for internal and external communication about environmental issues. The basic requirement Clause 4.3.3 is to establish and maintain procedures to:

- Communicate internally between the various levels and functions of the organization.
- Receive, document, and respond to "relevant communication from external interested parties" regarding environmental aspects and the EMS.

Open internal communication is critical to an effective EMS. This can include the results of EMS monitoring, audits, and management reviews. Internal communication of this type improves motivation, helps solve problems, and raises awareness. Therefore, the first requirement is straightforward.

External communication, however, can be a delicate matter and can lead to, among other things, liability problems. The same broad and open disclosure that results in discovering environmental problems and solving them may also create information that not all companies want to disclose externally. This is especially true for companies that operate in a regulatory environment, such as that of the United States, whose laws require disclosure of vast amounts of information already.

There are two modifiers in the requirement, namely that the communication be "relevant" and that it respond to "interested parties." The implication is that an organization decides what is relevant communication and thus it need not respond to everybody and anybody about any issue.

Environmental Reporting

The basic requirement to communicate with external interested parties in Clause 4.3.3 is reactive and passive: if someone requests relevant information, the organization must respond. Of course, as Annex A to ISO 14001 points out, external communication can result in a useful dialogue with interested parties and, in some cases, companies may include information about environmental impacts associated with their operations. And these procedures should include necessary communication with public authorities regarding issues such as emergency planning.

Clause 4.3.3 of ISO 14001 adds a requirement, however, that sounds more proactive when it requires the organization to *"consider* processes for external communication on its significant environmental aspects and record its decision." [Emphasis added.]

In contrast, the UK's BS 7750 and the EU's EMAS regulation require that companies publish a register of their significant environmental effects. (See Box.) ISO 14001 is not as prescriptive in this regard. Of course, many companies have instituted external reporting procedures. Many publish detailed environmental "annual reports." These reports often contain detailed information about environmental policies, objectives, and performance. And reporting is required for regulatory purposes. Companies also offer other methods for communication, such as 800-numbers for questions and complaints, company newsletters, and similar methods.

External reporting demonstrates management commitment, addresses questions and concerns proactively, and encourages acceptance of the company's environmental policies.

The Environmental Effects Register

The United Kingdom's BS 7750 EMS standard and the European Union's EMAS regulation require that companies compile a register of their significant environmental effects. These include such things as controlled and uncontrolled emissions to the atmosphere, controlled and uncontrolled discharges to water, solid and other wastes, use of land, water, fuels and energy and other natural resources, and other types of environmental effects.

Many delegations to TC 207 did not favor such a prescriptive approach to recording and communicating environmental effects. That's why the ISO/DIS 14001 standard only requires organizations to *consider* external communication of such environmental information but does not require it and why the Annex notes that companies "may include" information about environmental impacts.

External communication has been another hotly debated issue. The EMAS regulation requires the publication of a verified public environmental statement. Some delegations from the EU, as well as other regions of the world that want to use ISO 14001 registration as a way to increase public disclosure of environmental performance and thereby prod companies to improve, consider the external communication requirements in ISO 14001 as too weak.

EMS Documentation

The basic requirement in ISO 14001 in Clause 4.3.4 is to establish and maintain information that describes the "core elements of the management system and their interaction" and that provides "direction for related documentation." The information can be in paper or electronic form. The documentation provides a useful picture of the EMS.

The EMS documentation need not actually contain all operating procedures, instructions, or similar documents but can point users to where that information may be found. The related information can include internal operating procedures, internal standards, process information, work instructions, site emergency plans, records, and so on.

The Annex to ISO 14001 points out that the documentation should be detailed enough to describe the EMS. It can be integrated and shared with other information systems within the organization. It need not be another, separate layer nor need it be a single manual. Often, organizations create an EMS manual that provides the basics, such as the environmental policies, objectives, targets, key roles, and major responsibilities. The manual references related documentation and other aspects of the organization's management system.

An approach that has been generally favored in ISO 9000 quality management application is a documentation hierarchy, consisting of four layers or tiers. Each layer develops a steadily increasing level of detail about company operations and methods. These layers are shown in Figure 4–1 and consist of the following:

- The environmental manual.
- Company operating procedures.
- Work instructions.
- Records.

The layers in Figure 4–1 are presented as a broad-based triangle. The environmental manual would generally contain the basic policies, objectives and targets, and other general information about the EMS program. The operating procedures describe the overall flow of activities. Work

FIGURE 4–1
Documentation Hierarchy

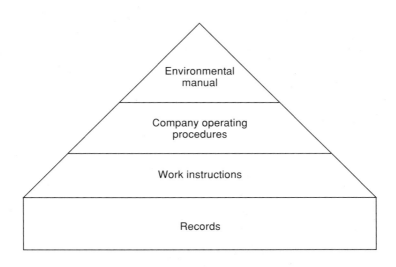

instructions are more detailed, activity-specific guidelines. And records include all documentation needed to demonstrate compliance with the EMS and its requirements.

Documentation has often been mentioned as one of the greatest challenges and obstacles in the ISO 9000 context. Companies implementing ISO 9000 standards have complained that it requires a "paper factory." If the ISO 9000 quality management system is implemented inefficiently, it can be nothing more than a paper exercise, with beautifully designed manuals that sit on a shelf gathering dust.

ISO 14000 implementation doesn't necessarily require reams of additional documentation, nor does it require documenting everything indiscriminately. It *does* require, however, that an organization document those aspects of its operations that demonstrate to an auditor that the system is in place and functioning effectively.

The Annex to ISO 14001 emphasizes the point that the primary focus is on effective implementation of the EMS, not on complex documentation systems developed for their own sake. In many cases, there may be similar or overlapping documentation requirements in the quality and environmental area. It makes sense to use the same documents where there is such overlap and where it is practical to do so.

Document Control

In the document control clause, 4.3.5, ISO 14001 requires the organization to set up clear procedures to control all documents required by the ISO 14001 standard. This includes procedures for creating and modifying documents.

Whatever the procedure, it must produce documents that:

- Can be located.
- Are legible, identifiable, dated (with dates of revision), and maintained in an orderly manner.
- Are periodically reviewed, revised, and approved for adequacy.
- Are updated and available to everyone who needs them, at all essential locations.
- Are maintained for a specified period and removed from use when obsolete.
- If obsolete, but retained for legal and/or auditor knowledge, are identified as such.

The organization must also develop procedures for creating and modifying various types of documents.

Operational Control

The next step in EMS implementation is operational control, Clause 4.3.6. The basic requirement is to identify and plan the activities and operations "associated with the identified significant environmental aspects in line with its policy, objectives, and targets." As described earlier, these activities were defined in the setting of policies, objectives, and targets, and range from R&D and product design, through production, marketing, customer service, and final product disposal.

The purpose of controls is to ensure that environmental performance meets the objectives and targets. Organizations achieve operational control by:

- Preparing documented procedures for the activities and operations to ensure that they do not deviate from policies, objectives, and targets.
- Specifying operating criteria.
- Establishing and communicating relevant procedures to suppliers and contractors that relate to the significant environmental aspects of goods and services used by the organization.

Again, documented procedures are not necessary for every operation and every circumstance, only to "cover situations where their absence could lead to deviations from the environmental policy and the objectives and targets."

Suppliers and Contractors

The ISO 9001 quality management standard requires companies to evaluate and select subcontractors on the basis of their ability to meet subcontract requirements.[6]

ISO 14001 doesn't focus on evaluating and selecting subcontractors but rather on communicating relevant procedures and requirements to contractors and suppliers. The specific requirement in Clause 4.3.6 is to establish and maintain "procedures related to the identifiable significant environmental aspects of goods and services used by the organization and communicating relevant procedures and requirements to suppliers and contractors."

This can mean communicating requirements for raw materials, procedures for proper disposal of waste products, storage procedures (if done off-site), and similar activities. Of course, if in the course of setting up an EMS, a company evaluates its raw materials usage and decides to substitute another raw material, this could involve selecting a new supplier.

Emergency Preparedness and Response

The organization must be ready to respond to abnormal operating conditions, accidents, and emergency situations. These can include, among other occurrences, accidental discharges to water and land, accidental emissions to the atmosphere, and other specific effects to the ecosystem from accidental releases.

The basic requirement in ISO 14001, Clause 4.3.7, is to establish and maintain procedures to identify the potential for and the response to accidents and emergency situations. The organization should also be prepared to prevent and mitigate associated environmental impacts. Finally, the organization must review and revise, when necessary, its emergency preparedness procedures and test them whenever practical.

The ISO 14004 guidance standard points out that emergency plans can include: assigning authority and responsibility, developing procedures for providing emergency services, methods to react to different types of emergencies, information on hazardous materials, internal and external emergency communication, and training for emergency preparedness and response. This should be related to existing company procedures for health and safety.

CHECKING AND CORRECTIVE ACTION

The next major aspect of implementing an EMS is to check and monitor the system, discover problems, and correct them. Clause 4.4 describes four general aspects of the process:

- Measure, monitor, and evaluate environmental performance.
- If problems occur, apply corrective and preventive action.
- Maintain environmental records to demonstrate conformance of the EMS to ISO 14001 requirements.
- Audit the environmental management system.

Monitoring and Measurement

A key idea behind environmental performance evaluation is the notion that "you can manage only what you can measure." Thus, the first basic requirement in checking and corrective action is establishing and maintaining documented procedures for regular monitoring and measurement of the key characteristics of the company's operations and activities. Again, these don't refer to all operations and activities but to those that significantly impact the environment.

The documented procedures required in Clause 4.4.1 of ISO 14001 include:

- Recording information to track performance, operational controls, and conformance with objectives and targets.
- Calibrating and maintaining monitoring equipment such as instruments, test equipment, software, and hardware sampling to ensure reliability.
- Maintaining calibration and maintenance records.
- Periodically evaluating compliance with relevant environmental legislation and regulations.

Relationship to environmental performance evaluation. The standards being developed by SC4 on EPE can provide a company with useful measurement tools. SC4 defines environmental performance evaluation as a "process to measure, analyze, assess, and describe an organization's environmental performance against agreed criteria for appropriate management purposes."

The EPE standards help companies identify appropriate environmental performance indicators. These are specific descriptions of performance, such as the volume of raw material per unit output or kg of air emissions per unit of production. These performance indicators provide input into the monitoring and measurement process and provide useful information to track performance.

Compliance audits. The requirement to evaluate compliance with legislation and regulations can be accomplished by environmental compliance auditing, as the term is understood in the United States. However, to maintain flexibility in EMS methods and also because the term *compliance auditing* does not necessarily refer to the same process worldwide, the standard does not specifically call for compliance auditing but for whatever procedure the organization needs to ensure "compliance with relevant environmental legislation and regulation."

Nonconformance and Corrective and Preventive Action

When problems occur, the organization must be prepared to correct them and to prevent recurrence. The focus is on root cause analysis, on the disease, not just the symptoms. The idea is not just to identify the problem but to understand why it occurred and to change the system so that it does not recur.

The basic requirements in ISO 14001, Clause 4.4.2, include procedures for:

- Defining responsibility and authority for handling and investigating nonconformances.
- Acting to mitigate the resulting impacts on the environment.
- Initiating and completing corrective and preventive action.
- Implementing and recording changes to documented procedures that result from corrective and preventive action.

The standard states that corrective or preventive actions "taken to eliminate the causes of actual and potential nonconformances shall be appropriate to the magnitude of problems and commensurate with the environmental impact encountered." Thus, the procedures can be simple or complex, broad or narrow in scope, depending upon the problem.

Records

The organization must maintain appropriate records to demonstrate conformance to the requirements of the standard. This means developing procedures for identifying, maintaining, and disposing of environmental records. According to ISO 14001, Clause 4.4.3, environmental records include "training records and the results of audits and reviews."

As the ISO 14004 guidance standard states, records are evidence of the ongoing operation of the EMS. Records can include, in addition to the above:

- Legislative and regulatory requirements.
- Inspection, maintenance, and calibration records.

- Incident reports.
- Reports of environmental audits and reviews.
- Contractor and supplier information.
- Emergency response records.

The standard points out that environmental records must be "legible, identifiable, traceable . . . readily retrievable and protected against damage, deterioration, or loss." The organization must also establish and record retention times for records.[7]

The Annex to ISO 14001 also mentions that companies should take into account confidential business information in the records management process.

Every environmental manager is aware of the vast amount and complex range of information that an EMS produces. To some extent, effective environmental management is good information management. There is a trend to create electronic environmental information management systems to keep track of all the data. Discussion of these methods goes beyond the scope of this book. Suffice it to say that implementing ISO 14000 can be made more effective with efficient use of information technology.

Environmental Management System Audit

Periodically, the organization must examine the EMS to make sure it works. In Clause 4.4.4, ISO 14001 requires the company to carry out audits of the environmental management system. This is a *system* audit, not an audit for technical compliance with laws and regulations.

The aim is to make sure the EMS "conforms to planned arrangements for environmental management including the requirements of this standard," and has been properly implemented and maintained. The other aim of the EMS audit is to provide information on its results to management.

The standard also emphasizes that the audit program and its scheduled frequency must be based on the "environmental importance of the activity concerned and the results of previous audits."

The audit procedures should be comprehensive and cover the scope of the audit, its frequency, and its methods. They should also cover responsibilities and requirements for conducting audits and reporting results.

Annex A to ISO 14001 adds that the procedures should also cover auditor competence. It also points out that organizations can conduct audits using internal or external personnel. In either case, the auditors should be impartial and objective. System audits for ISO 9000 and ISO 14001 can be performed at the same time, where possible. EMS auditing is discussed in more detail in Chapter 6.

MANAGEMENT REVIEW

The final step in the basic EMS process is to review the EMS itself. The basic requirement in Clause 4.5 of ISO 14001 calls on top management to review the EMS, whenever it determines appropriate, "to ensure its continuing suitability, adequacy, and effectiveness." Management must make sure it has collected the information necessary for a comprehensive evaluation and that it documents the review.

The review looks at the EMS audit results, at changing circumstances, and the organization's commitment to continual improvement and addresses possible changes in policy, objectives, and other EMS elements.

Annex A points out that not all components of the EMS need to be reviewed at once and that the review process may take place over a period of time. The Annex also points out that reviews of policies, objectives, and procedures should be carried out by the level of management that defined them.

The "changing circumstances" referred to in the clause can include changes in legislation, varying expectations of interested parties, changes in the organization's products or activities, technological advances, marketing information, and feedback from environmental incidents.

To complete the circle of continual improvement, management should plan corrective and preventive action to improve the EMS and should follow up to ensure the actions were taken and were effective. The results of the management review may dictate changes in the environmental policy which would trigger changes in the EMS itself.

Management Review versus EMS Audit

One final point about the relationship between the EMS audit and the management review. They are not the same thing. The auditors conducting the EMS audit, whether internal or external, can include conclusions about improving the EMS in their reports, if management asks for them. It is not generally the auditor's job to review the EMS itself, however. This is the job of top management, using information from the audit, from the environmental performance evaluation system, and any other sources necessary to make good decisions.

This relationship between the EMS audit and top management review is discussed in Chapter 6, in the context of the ISO auditing standards.

CONCLUSION

The ISO/DIS 14001 standard is relatively short. The primary clauses are no more than nine pages long. The requirements are straightforward and deceptively simple. Companies that already have well-developed management systems in place will be well along the road to complying with ISO 14001 requirements. Companies with less-developed systems may take longer to implement the requirements. Although it is beyond the scope of this book to offer extensive implementation guidance, Chapter 12 provides some suggestions to help organizations get started.

NOTES

1. There is some difference of opinion regarding the role of ISO 14004, even among the standards developers. The standard is not designed to give the impression that implementing ISO 14004 results in a system that is superior to, or exceeds, ISO 14001. According to this view, ISO 14004 isn't "better" than ISO 14001 nor does it necessarily describe an "environmental excellence program" that goes beyond the basics of ISO 14001. The ISO 14001 standard contains all the necessary elements of an effective EMS program.

2. As explained in Chapter 7 on environmental performance evaluation, it is possible to have environmental performance without an environmental management system or to measure performance without developing an EMS.

3. Although the generic standard is designed to apply to all types and sizes of businesses, it remains to be seen whether small to medium-size enterprises (SMEs) will find the standard appealing or useful.

4. The degree to which environmental improvement should be made explicit in the standard has been the source of much debate. Delegates from Europe have sought to include a more explicit requirement for environmental performance in the ISO 14001 standard, to make it

correspond more closely to the EU's EMAS regulation. Even though the standard is in DIS form, the issue of environmental performance will remain a source of debate.

5. The presence of BAT in Annex A of ISO 14001 is the result of a compromise between those in TC 207 who favored its inclusion in the actual specification and those who considered it a performance requirement and therefore wanted it removed. The EMAS regulation in the European Union, however, requires the use of EVABAT. This is discussed in more detail in Chapter 5.

6. *ANSI/ASQC Q9001—1994 Quality systems—model for quality assurance in design, development, production, installation, and servicing.* Clause 4.6.2 Evaluation of subcontractors.

7. Some delegations to TC 207 recommended adding records of significant environmental releases and impacts, based on the rationale that if no records on releases exist, the environmental verifier or auditor cannot estimate the validity of the reported environmental impacts. Again, this idea relates to EMAS requirements for a register of environmental effects, described in the next chapter.

Chapter Five

The Eco-Management and Audit Scheme

As mentioned in the first chapter, companies are already registering facilities to the UK's BS 7750 EMS standard, and companies with EU sites are developing EMS and auditing programs that will fulfill the requirements of the Eco-Management and Audit Scheme (EMAS) regulation. How are ISO 14000, BS 7750, and EMAS similar? How do they differ? How do they fit together? A detailed discussion of every EMS-related initiative goes beyond the scope of this book. This chapter, however, briefly describes EMAS, a regional initiative that has affected the development and timetable of ISO 14000 and may affect how organizations implement EMS programs for sites located in one of the member states of the European Union. In addition, Appendix A includes a matrix that compares the UK's BS 7750 standard, EMAS, and ISO 9001 with ISO 14001 requirements. Appendix B describes the EMAS requirements in greater detail.

THE EUROPEAN UNION AND ENVIRONMENTAL PROTECTION

A major factor in the development of EMAS has been the formation of the European Union (EU) and the nature of the European Union's approach to environmental regulation.

A key goal of the EU's 1992 initiative was to expand trade in the European Union and to reduce trade barriers among the member states. At the same time, along with other regions of the world, the EU faces environmental challenges. Environmental protection and enforcement in the European Union varies by member state. In response to environmental concerns, the EU has been looking for communitywide solutions to complement national legislation. (The enforcement of environmental legislation, whether it is developed at the EU level or at the national level, is enforced at the national level.)

The goal is to develop EU-wide environmental policies that protect the environment but allow for free trade and regional differences. The ultimate aim is to work toward sustainable development. To achieve this goal, the EU is looking beyond the traditional "command and control" approach to environmental regulation. Alternatives include various market-based programs that reward environmentally responsible behavior by industry and bring public attention and pressure to bear on environmental problems. Such approaches can also improve the enforcement of environmental laws and reduce the high cost of environmental regulation and enforcement.

The main obstacle to EU-wide approaches is that the EU legislative system is weak and can't do much to enforce environmental protection at the member state level. It is difficult for the EU to pass detailed legislation; and once adopted, such legislation is difficult to enforce. Thus, the EU is looking for other ways to achieve its environmental goals. The voluntary EMAS scheme is one such method.

Development of the European Union

The full members of the European Union are Austria, Belgium, Denmark, Finland, France, Germany, Greece, Ireland, Italy, Luxembourg, the Netherlands, Portugal, Spain, Sweden, and the UK. The European Union (EU) originated with the 1957 Treaty of Rome, which was established to abolish tariffs and quotas among its six member states and to stimulate economic growth in Europe. Differing national product certification requirements, however, made selling products in multiple national markets in the European Community a costly and complex process. In addition, Europe feared that competition from the United States and the Pacific Rim would slow European economic growth.

In response, the EU called for a greater push toward a Single Internal Market and for the removal of physical, technical, and fiscal barriers to trade. In 1985, the EC Commission presented a program for establishing a single internal market, and this goal was further expedited by the Single European Act, adopted in February 1986. The goal of this legislation was to abolish barriers to trade among the member states and to complete an

(Continued)

(Continued)

internal European market by the end of 1992. The single market became effective at midnight on December 31, 1992.

The Single European Act of 1986 also recognized the EU's involvement in environmental matters by adding environmental chapters to the original treaties. By 1993, up to 400 separate items of European environmental legislation had been developed and more than 200 pieces of legislation have been adopted so far in the field of environmental protection.

EU Standards and Regional Standardization Organizations

A key goal of the European Union is to develop EU-wide, harmonized standards to replace differing national standards. EU legislation, such as the EMAS regulation, does not contain such standards but references them instead. The task of developing specific standards is carried out primarily by three European standard-setting organizations. These include the Committee for European Standardization (or Normalization, hence the "N" in CEN), the European Committee for Electrotechnical Standardization (CENELEC), and the European Telecommunications Standards Institute (ETSI).

These organizations develop standards according to priorities set by the European Union and its member states. They also consult with existing national and international standardization organizations. CEN and CENELEC have negotiated agreements with the two international standards organizations, ISO and International Electrotechnical Committee (IEC), to develop new standards.

CEN is composed of delegates from the national standardization organizations of 18 European countries. CENELEC is CEN's sister organization. While CEN works closely with ISO, CENELEC works with its international counterpart, the IEC. The European Telecommunications Standardization Institute (ETSI) promotes European standards for a unified telecommunications system.

The procedures for developing CENELEC standards and CEN standards are similar. Published European standards are referred to as EN standards (for European Norms). CEN and CENELEC will develop a new standard when:

- A standard does not already exist under ISO or IEC auspices.
- The standard cannot be developed at the international level.

(Continued)

(Continued)

- The standard cannot be developed at the international level within a specific time frame.

All member states are obligated to adopt an EN standard as their national standard by withdrawing the conflicting national standard. If the ISO 14000 standards are adopted by the European Union, they will be adopted as EN standards, just as the ISO 9000 series was adopted as the EN 29000 series by the European Union.

THE ECO-MANAGEMENT AND AUDIT SCHEME (EMAS)

The first draft of the Eco-Management and Audit Scheme regulation was first released in December 1990. It was conceived as a mandatory requirement that was to apply to the most polluting industries in the EU. After protests from the companies and sites affected about the mandatory nature of the regulation, it was revised in March 1992 and became a voluntary scheme. EMAS entered into force in July 1993 as "Council regulation (EEC) No. 1836/93 allowing voluntary participation by companies in the industrial sector in a Community eco-management and audit scheme."[1] The EMAS regulation opened for participation on April 10, 1995.

It is a communitywide scheme that allows voluntary participation by industrial companies for the evaluation and improvement of their environmental performance and the provision of relevant information to the public.

Basic Purpose

EMAS makes adherence to a formal environmental management system and auditing mandatory and requires that organizations make independently verifiable public statements regarding their environmental performance. Participation in the program entitles a company to register a site on an EU-authorized list of participating sites and to use an EU-approved statement of participation and graphic to publicize inclusion in the program.

The specific objectives of EMAS are to:

- Promote continuous improvements in environmental performance by establishing policies, programs, and management systems.

- Perform systematic, objective, and periodic evaluation of these elements.
- Provide relevant information about these activities to the public.

Voluntary or Mandatory?

Although the program is currently voluntary, EU firms, as well as non–EU-based companies with EU sites, are concerned that EMAS could become mandatory. The EC's Environmental Commission hopes market pressures will act as an inducement. Within five years of the regulation coming into force (1998), the Commission will review the scheme in particular to consider extending the scope of the scheme and the introduction of a logo. At this time the Commission may review participation in the scheme and decide whether to make it compulsory.

As an EC regulation, EMAS is directly applicable in the national laws of the member states. Each EU member state is required to set up a structure to allow for EMAS participation.

Applies to Industrial Firms

Participation in the scheme is site-based and open to companies operating industrial activities as defined in the EU's NACE classification of industries. (This is similar to the Standard Industrial Classification Code.) In addition to manufacturing industries, the scheme also applies to the electrical, gas, steam and waste disposal sectors. Within the Regulation, a facility exists for the EU Member States to extend the scheme's provisions on an experimental basis to other sectors. This type of experimental application is already under way in the areas of local government and rail and air transport. It is possible that, in due course, more areas will be covered by these national extensions of the scheme, such as retail industries, tourism, banking, central government, and so on.

Reasons to Participate

In addition to the possibility that EMAS may become mandatory, another reason to participate is market pressure. Organizations with European sites may be encouraged to participate for competitive reasons and to achieve recognition in the EU marketplace. Organizations that choose not to seek ISO 14001 registration for non-European sites may nevertheless register their EU sites to ISO 14001 as part of EMAS participation.

Another reason is the possible role of EMAS participation in public procurement. The Dutch government has already started giving preference to companies that are registered to an EMS standard as a condition for receiving construction and operating permits. The UK's Ministry of Defense is watching EMS progress closely to determine if it is practical to require suppliers to be registered to EMAS, BS 7750, or ISO 14001. Municipal governments in the United Kingdom are getting involved in EMAS participation.

A number of member states are considering the "deregulatory" potential of EMAS—participation in the scheme is likely to mean fewer inspection visits by the regulators, more rapid processing of license applications, reduced licensing fees, and so forth. If and when confidence in the scheme builds, the scope for "deregulatory" initiatives will increase. In developing EMAS, the European Commission's view is that it is giving an opportunity for industry to demonstrate that the voluntary approach to regulation in the field of environment is effective. For many years, much of industry has asked for a more flexible approach and for fewer command and control instruments. By participating in EMAS they have an opportunity to modify the pattern of regulation, away from command and control and voluntary and flexible instruments.

CEN's Vote to Select a Standard to Support EMAS

EMAS is designed as a stand-alone scheme. That is, companies can meet the requirements of EMAS and seek verification of compliance with EMAS without implementing other EMS standards and achieving registration.

Article 12 of the EMAS regulation, *Relationship with national, European and international standards,* however, offers organizations another option. It states that companies that have implemented national, European, or international standards for environmental management systems and audits and are certified to one of these standards would be considered to meet the corresponding requirements of the EMAS regulation. For example, a company registered to ISO 14001 would be considered to fulfill the EMS requirements in EMAS.

The EC commission has issued a mandate to the Committee for European Standardization (CEN) to produce or adopt existing standards to support EMAS.

The expectation is that CEN will recognize ISO 14001 as largely meeting EMAS requirements. Some of the differences in the approach between EMAS and the ISO 14001 standard may be resolved by a "bridge" or interpretive document. This document would describe the requirements EU sites aiming for EMAS participation would have to meet in addition to those in ISO 14001 to bridge the differences between EMAS and ISO 14001.[2]

CEN is also working on auditing standards that would be acceptable for EMAS.

General requirements of EMAS

This section is a brief synopsis of EMAS requirements. Where appropriate, it points out differences between ISO 14001 and EMAS requirements. (Appendix B includes a more detailed description of EMAS requirements.)

EMAS calls for firms to establish management systems and programs to periodically and systematically audit their environmental performance, to strive for continuous improvement and to inform the public of their results.

EMAS consists of 21 Articles and 5 Annexes. (It should be noted that, unlike international standards where annexes are largely informative, the annexes of EMAS form part of the Regulation and are mandatory for those participating in the scheme.) The detailed requirements start with Article 3. The scheme is open to companies that implement the following requirements.

ADOPT AN ENVIRONMENTAL POLICY

The company must adopt a company environmental policy that provides for compliance with all regulatory requirements regarding the environment and includes a commitment to achieve "reasonable continuous improvement of environmental performance, with a view to reducing environmental impacts to levels not exceeding those corresponding to economically viable application of best available technology."

Note that this requirement, unlike ISO 14001, is performance-oriented and refers explicitly to EVABAT. The issue of best available technology was mentioned in ISO 14001, but only in the informative Annex.

EMAS prescribes several principles on which the environmental policy must be based, including among others, assessing the environmental impact of all current activities, implementing pollution prevention, providing information to the public about the environmental impact of the company's activities, and providing advice to customers about the environmental aspects of the handling, use, and disposal of its products.

EMAS also prescribes a list of issues that the policy, EMS program, and audits must address, including energy management, environmental impact reduction, raw materials management, waste avoidance, product planning, and so on.

CONDUCT AN ENVIRONMENTAL REVIEW

EMAS calls for an initial environmental review that focuses on the issues addressed by the environmental policy. This sets the stage for the EMS system. Of course, if the organization already has an EMS system in place, its environmental review would not be initial but would likely check to make sure it addresses the issues described in EMAS.

SET ENVIRONMENTAL OBJECTIVES

Like ISO 14001, EMAS requires the company to specify environmental objectives at all relevant levels within the company that are consistent with its policies. The objectives must be set "at the highest appropriate management level, aimed at the continuous improvement of environmental performance . . ." Based on findings from the audit, EMAS requires management to set higher objectives and to revise the environmental program to be able to achieve those objectives. This step is analogous to the management review of ISO 14001.

INTRODUCE AN ENVIRONMENTAL PROGRAM AND EMS

In light of the results of the environmental review, the company sets up an environmental program applicable to all activities at the site and aimed at achieving the commitments in the environmental policy. In general, these requirements are similar to those in ISO 14001.

Environmental Effects Register

EMAS requires the company to examine and assess the environmental effects of its activities at the site and compile a register of significant effects. This register is not required in ISO 14001.

The company must also establish and maintain procedures to record all legislative, regulatory, and other policy requirements pertaining to the environmental aspects of its activities, products, and services.

SET UP AN ENVIRONMENTAL AUDITING PROGRAM

EMAS prescribes detailed auditing requirements. It calls for the organization to set up, implement, and revise a systematic and periodic program of environmental audits concerning:

- Whether or not the environmental management activities conform to the environmental program and are implemented effectively.
- How effective the EMS is in fulfilling the company's environmental policy.

It must then carry out or cause to be carried out environmental audits at the site. The audits may be conducted by either company auditors or external auditors acting on the company's behalf.

EMAS requires that the audit frequency or the audit cycle is completed at intervals of no longer than three years.

PREPARE AN ENVIRONMENTAL STATEMENT

The company must prepare an environmental statement "specific to each site audited." This is done upon completion of the initial environmental review and subsequent audits or audit cycles. This public environmental statement and its validation is a key goal of the entire EMAS effort. (See Appendix B for details of what the statement must contain.)

After the first statement is issued, companies must produce simplified annual statements in the intervening years between the audits. There are two exceptions: where the nature and scale of the operations are such that no additional statements are necessary until the next audit, and where there have been few significant changes since the last environmental statement.

VERIFICATION AND VALIDATION

The company must have its policy, program, management system, review, or audit program examined by an external accredited verifier and the environmental statement(s) validated to ensure that they meet the requirements of EMAS. The verifier is "any person or organization independent of the company being verified" who is accredited. Regarding verification, the verifier checks whether:

- The environmental policy has been established and whether it meets the requirements of EMAS.
- An EMS is in place at the site, in operation, and that it complies with relevant EMAS requirements.
- The environmental review and audit is carried out in accordance with EMAS requirements.
- The data and information in the environmental statement are reliable and whether the statement adequately covers all the significant and relevant environmental issues. If so, the statement is validated.

Verifier Does Not Duplicate Company's Internal Procedures

Does the verifier come in and re-do the company's audit? Not as envisioned. The verifier does not duplicate, substitute for, or complement the company's internal assessment procedures. Basically, the verifier "investigates" in a sound professional manner the technical validity of the environmental review or audit or other procedures carried out by the company, without unnecessarily duplicating those procedures. The verifier examines documentation before visiting the site. At the site, the verifier interviews personnel and prepares a report to the company management that specifies:

- In general, cases of noncompliance with the provisions of EMAS.

- Technical defects in the environmental review, or audit method, or environmental management system, or any other relevant process.
- Points of disagreement with the draft environmental statement and details of the amendments or additions that should be made to the environmental statement.

If the environmental policy has not been established, or the environmental review or audit is not technically satisfactory, or the environmental program or EMS doesn't meet EMAS requirements, the verifier makes appropriate recommendations to the company's management and will not validate the environmental statement until the problems have been corrected.

If the only problem is that the environmental statement must be revised, the verifier discusses the changes with the company management and will validate the statement when the company makes the appropriate additions and/or amendments.

Sites That Are Registered to an EMS Standard

In cases where the site has been registered to an EMS standard, such as ISO 14001, the verifier limits verification to confirming the validity of the EMS certification, checking the environmental policies and programs, reviewing the audit procedures, and examining the environmental statement to ensure that it is complete, fair, and balanced in light of the results from the internal audit and internal monitoring procedures. The verifier examines the conclusions from the internal audit concerning compliance with the regulation's requirements, including the environmental policy and its conformity with the company's objectives and standards.

If the company does not have an EMS in place and wants to participate in EMAS, the verifier will perform a dual role: audit the facility against the requirements of EMAS (as described above) and perform the verification and validation process.

DISTRIBUTE AND DISSEMINATE THE ENVIRONMENTAL STATEMENT

The company forwards the validated environmental statement to the competent body of the member state where the site is located and disseminates it as appropriate to the public in that state after the site is registered. (See Box for description of a competent authority.)

SITE REGISTRATION

Site registration occurs when the competent body, designated by the member state, receives a validated environmental statement, levies a registration fee, and is satisfied the site meets the regulation's requirements, including compliance with all relevant environmental legislation. What happens if the verifier doesn't validate the statement? The company must take action to remedy audit defaults and/or noncompliance reports/presentation defaults.

LISTING OF THE REGISTRATION

Each year, the lists of registered sites from the 15 member states will be communicated to the commission and a complete list published in the *Official Journal of the European Union.* To promote their involvement in the scheme, companies can use a graphic symbol linked to a statement of participation which lists the site, within a company, that is registered to the scheme. It cannot be used in product advertising or on products or their packaging. The graphic symbol cannot be used on its own.

What Is a Competent Authority?

Each member state of the EU is responsible for designating an independent and neutral competent body within 12 months of the EMAS regulation entering into force. A competent authority or competent body is the national authority in each member country that has overall responsibility for the oversight of the scheme, the registration of sites and maintenance of the register. A competent body can be either a government agency or independent organization that has the authority to recognize accreditation bodies. For example, in the United Kingdom, the Department of the Environment has been designated as the competent body. A number of member states have also designated the duty of informing companies in the member state of the Regulation and informing the public of the objectives and principles of the EMAS regulation.

SUMMARY—BASIC DIFFERENCES BETWEEN EMAS AND ISO 14000

Now that we've described the requirements of EMAS, it's useful to point out the basic differences between ISO 14001 and EMAS requirements. The most obvious difference is that EMAS is a voluntary regulation while ISO 14001 is an international standard. Thus, where EMAS applies only to sites within the EU, ISO 14001 is applicable worldwide. Other key differences include the following:

- EMAS is site-specific and relates to industrial activities whereas ISO 14001 applies to activities, products, and services across all sectors, including nonindustrial activities such as government. Note, however, that under EMAS, nonindustrial activities are being included on an experimental basis.

- EMAS requires an extensive initial environmental review as part of the EMS. This is not specifically required in ISO 14001, although it is suggested in Annex 4.2.1 of ISO 14001.

- As mentioned above, EMAS focuses more directly on the improvement of environmental performance than does ISO 14001, which places more emphasis on establishing and improving the EMS, with environmental performance improvement as an implied but not prescribed consequence.[3]

- EMAS requires the publication of a validated public environmental statement and an annual simplified statement. ISO 14001 does not require a public statement. In Clause 4.3.3, it simply calls on companies to consider external communication. It is up to the company to decide what information and how much to communicate. In addition, while EMAS requires the company to make publicly available its policies, programs, and EMS system, ISO 14001 requires only the environmental policy to be made available to the public.

- EMAS appears to call for more extensive auditing than does ISO 14001, which requires only EMS auditing. (Although the organization under ISO 14001 must periodically evaluate compliance with its requirements).

- EMAS, unlike ISO 14001, specifies a maximum audit frequency of three years.
- The EMS requirements in EMAS call for the preparation of an environmental effects register, which is not required in ISO 14001.

CONCLUSION

Since the EMAS regulation is new and the system for verification and validation is only now being set up, many issues surrounding EMAS implementation will be resolved only through application. Sites in Europe that are implementing EMAS cannot have their participation certified until EMAS criteria are published. (As this book goes to print, the first EMAS verifiers and registered sites are beginning to appear on the registers of the EU member states and the European Commission.)

It remains to be seen how broadly the EMAS regulation is adopted by companies with EU sites. Many EU delegations to the ISO 14000 development process lobbied for language in ISO 14001 that draws it closer to EMAS requirements. And countries such as Germany, among others, are looking at EMAS participation to ease the regulatory burdens on industry. These and other countries may vote to make EMAS a legislative requirement in the future, rather than a voluntary scheme.

A few key issues to be resolved regarding EMAS include the following:

- The exact nature and scope of the activities performed by the EMAS verifier.
- The experience and qualifications required of an effective EMAS verifier.
- The precise applicability of ISO 14001 and the ISO 14010–12 auditing standards within the EMAS context.
- The possibility that EMAS, if adopted as a de facto marketplace requirement in the EU, might pose a trade barrier to companies with non-EU sites.
- The nature of the continual improvement of performance specified by EMAS.

In the meantime, companies with sites in Europe that may be interested in EMAS participation should examine the EMAS regulation in detail, and monitor developments in the European Union.

NOTES

1. *The Official Journal of the European Communities,* no. L 168/1–18 (July 10, 1993).

2. The "bridge" document may consist of references to suggestions contained in Annex A of ISO/DIS 14001. The bridge document may make these suggestions requirements for the purposes of EMAS participation. One example would be the initial environmental review suggested in Annex A.

3. In the negotiations leading up to the acceptance of ISO 14001 as a Draft International Standard, some delegations from the European Union sought to make the standard more comparable to the EMAS regulation. Much of this effort played out in the definitions of concepts such as continual improvement and environmental performance. There was the concern among European delegates that the existing ISO 14001 is too weak for use in the EMAS system and that it should be more prescriptive and explicit in demanding environmental performance improvement. This is the reason that certain aspects of the EMAS regulation are referenced as suggestions in the Annex to ISO 14001. At minimum, TC 207 sought to minimize any contradictions between ISO 14001 and EMAS.

Chapter Six

Auditing the Environmental Management System

The ISO 14001 specification standard calls for organizations to perform environmental management system auditing to determine whether the EMS conforms to requirements and has been properly implemented. ISO 14001 also requires some procedure for periodically evaluating compliance with environmental legislation and regulations.

Subcommittee 2's work on environmental auditing will offer organizations useful guidance in meeting these objectives. If successful, SC2's standards will lead to a better understanding of environmental auditing and more consistency in auditing practices worldwide.

DEVELOPMENT OF ENVIRONMENTAL AUDITING

As with environmental management, it's useful to set the context for SC2's work by briefly tracing the history of environmental auditing, at least as it has developed in the United States.

Partly in response to government regulation, many companies starting in the 1970s began to look for ways to systematically evaluate their compliance with environmental requirements and also to assess the potential liabilities they faced as a result of noncompliance. Although in some cases audits were mandated by regulatory authorities, in most cases they were undertaken voluntarily by managers who wanted to identify problems and correct them, thus avoiding fines, penalties, and civil and criminal liability.

The growth of environmental auditing was spurred not only by regulatory pressures but also by highly publicized environmental accidents and violations that focused company attention on better managing environmental responsibilities.

The practice of environmental auditing continued to develop throughout the 1980s and early 1990s. Partly this was a result of encouragement by the EPA but also because environmental managers recognized its usefulness. Today, environmental auditing is the most widely accepted environmental management system tool.

In response, procedures, guidelines, and standards were developed by professional organizations such as the Environmental Auditing Roundtable, consulting firms such as Arthur D. Little, and by various standards organizations, including among others the American Society for Testing and Materials (ASTM) and the Canadian Standards Association.

WHAT IS ENVIRONMENTAL AUDITING?

Despite this increasing activity, organizations have differing ideas as to what constitutes environmental auditing. In 1986, the EPA developed a definition of environmental auditing as a "systematic, documented, periodic, and objective review by regulated entities of facility operations and practices related to meeting environmental requirements."[1]

Although to most US companies the term *environmental auditing* usually refers to compliance auditing, auditing according to the EPA definition can meet several objectives, including:

- Verifying compliance with environmental laws and regulations.
- Evaluating the effectiveness of systems already in place to manage environmental responsibilities.
- Assessing the risks from regulated and unregulated activities and facility operations.

SCOPE OF SUBCOMMITTEE 2

All of the above objectives fall within the scope of SC2's work. Its official scope is "standardization in the field of environmental auditing and related environmental investigations." This is a broad statement that can cover not only compliance (or performance) auditing and EMS auditing, but also areas such as site assessments, initial reviews, environmental statements, decommissioning audits, and other evaluative activities.

For example, Work Group 4 is looking at a possible standard for environmental site assessments. Other potential projects could focus on conducting initial environmental reviews and the management of environmental audit programs.

Subcommittee 2 is divided into four work groups.

Work Group 1 (WG1) is developing a standard on general principles of all environmental auditing. *ISO/DIS 14010 Guidelines for environmental auditing—General principles of environmental auditing* describes general principles common to all types of environmental auditing.

Work Group 2 (WG2) is looking at specific auditing procedures for various types of audits. The first standard to be issued from WG2, *ISO/DIS 14011/1 Guidelines for environmental auditing—Audit procedures—Part 1: Auditing of environmental management systems,* describes procedures for auditing environmental management systems. WG2 may also, in the future, consider standards for other types of audits.

Work Group 3 (WG3) is developing a standard, *ISO/DIS 14012 Guidelines for environmental auditing—Qualification criteria for environmental auditors,* that sets out qualifications for environmental auditors.

And Work Group 4 (WG4) has proposed a standard on environmental site assessments.

The ISO/DIS 14010–12 standards should be published by mid-1996, on a schedule parallel to that of the ISO 14001 specification standard.

Applicability

The standards apply to any type of environmental audit, whether conducted internally or commissioned externally. They can be used internally (first-party), in contract situations (second-party), and for external, third-party audits. And they apply to all types of organizations. Any company can use the guidance in the ISO/DIS 14010–12 series to set up its auditing program. Third-party registrars can also use the standards as guidance to conduct registration audits.

Guidance, Not Specifications

The ISO 14010–14012 series are guidance, not specification standards. They offer useful advice but are not designed for third-party registration of a company's auditing procedures.

The third standard in the series, ISO 14012, may be used more formally. It may be officially adopted by registrars and other groups as criteria for evaluating the work of environmental auditors. This is similar to the adoption of the ISO 10011 series of quality system auditing standards by quality system registrars and other organizations.

Also, recall from the previous chapter that CEN has been tasked with developing or adopting acceptable auditing standards to meet the auditing requirements of EMAS. The ISO 14010–12 series are likely to meet this requirement.

Not Required by ISO 14001

Although ISO 14001, in Clause 4.4.4, requires EMS audits, these audits need not be performed in conformance to the ISO 14011/1 EMS auditing procedures standard. A company can select ISO 14011/1 to guide its EMS audit program, but this is not an express requirement of ISO 14001. In a third-party audit of the EMS for registration purposes, the auditor should not evaluate the organization's auditing procedures for compliance to ISO 14010's principles or to ISO 14011/1's requirements. In short, the requirements of the ISO 14010–12 should not be subsumed into ISO 14001 requirements.

ISO/DIS 14010—GUIDELINES FOR ENVIRONMENTAL AUDITING

ISO 14010 defines key terms and describes some general principles for the environmental auditing process. ISO/DIS 14010 defines an environmental audit as a "systematic, documented verification process of objectively obtaining and evaluating audit evidence to determine whether specified environmental activities, events, conditions, management systems, or information about these matters conform with audit criteria, and communicating the results of this process to the client." The definition of an EMS audit is the same, except that the determination is limited to "whether an organization's environmental management system conforms with the environmental management system audit criteria."

Objective, Verifiable Audit Evidence

The purpose of any audit is to obtain and evaluate objective evidence that the audit criteria have been met. This refers to verifiable information, records, or statements of fact. It's typically based on interviews, examining documents, direct observation, and the results of testing, measurements, or other such methods.

What is quality audit evidence? ISO 14010 offers a very general yardstick: Audit evidence should be of such quality and quantity that competent auditors working independently with the same evidence would reach the same findings against the same audit criteria.

Conformance, Not Performance

Using the audit evidence, the auditor evaluates whether "specified environmental activities, events, conditions, management systems" conform to the audit criteria. In the case of an EMS audit, that means checking to make sure the EMS includes all the basic elements required by ISO 14001: Is there an environmental policy? Has the organization established objectives and targets? Is an environmental management in place that can achieve those objectives? And so on.

It does not mean checking the actual *performance* of the system. Nor is it, in the view of several delegations to the ISO 14000 drafting process, the auditor's primary task to judge the effectiveness or suitability of the EMS. This is the task for management, during the management review stage. In short, the auditor checks conformance; management evaluates performance.[2]

Findings versus Conclusions

According to ISO 14010, audit findings are "results of the evaluation of the collected audit evidence compared against the agreed audit criteria." The note to the definition adds that audit findings provide the basis for the audit report. Audit conclusions, however, are professional judgments or opinions "expressed by an auditor about the subject matter of the audit, based on and limited to reasoning the auditor has applied to audit findings."

The emphasis of the auditing standards is on developing audit findings, not conclusions. Several delegations to SC2 sought to minimize subjectivity by auditors and focus, instead, on gathering objective evidence of conformance.

The aim of the audit is to ensure confidence in the reliability of the audit findings and conclusions. ISO 14010 warns that audit evidence contains some element of uncertainty; it is, after all, only a sample, a "snapshot" of the organization's activities, since it's performed during a limited period and with limited resources. The standard urges auditors to take these limitations into account in planning the audit, executing the procedures, and evaluating the findings.

Audit Criteria

It's essential in an audit to develop appropriately detailed audit criteria, which include well-defined, written "policies, practices, procedures, or requirements against which the auditor compares collected audit evidence about the subject matter." Audit criteria may include but are not limited to standards, guidelines, specified organizational requirements, and legislative or regulatory requirements. It's up to the auditor and the client commissioning the audit to set the audit criteria and communicate them to the auditee.

In the case of an EMS audit, the audit criteria include "policies, practices, procedures, or requirements, such as covered by ISO 14001 and, if applicable, any additional EMS requirements." (ISO/DIS 14011/1)

In the standard, the client is defined as the "organization commissioning the audit." This may be the organization being audited (the auditee) but it can also be "any other organization which has the regulatory or contractual right to commission an audit."

Clearly Defined Subject Matter

An environmental audit should focus on clearly defined and documented subject matter. The party or parties responsible for the subject matter of the audit should also be clearly defined and documented.

The audit should be undertaken only if the auditor believes that there is:

- Sufficient or appropriate information about the subject matter.
- Adequate resources to support the audit process.
- Adequate cooperation from the auditee.

If these elements are missing or incomplete, the audit should not go forward.

Objectivity, Independence, and Competence

Auditors should be objective, unbiased, and free from conflict of interest. To ensure this, the members of the audit team should be independent of the activities they audit. Does this imply only external auditors? Not necessarily. The client organization can use either internal or external audit team members. But an internal auditor should not be accountable to those directly responsible for the subject matter being audited.

Needless to say, the auditor should be competent and possess appropriate knowledge, skills, and experience. This means meeting the qualifications for knowledge, skills, and experience described in ISO/DIS 14012. It also means ensuring quality by applying the auditing standards consistently and seeking authoritative interpretations when necessary.

ISO/DIS 14010 calls for auditors to exercise due professional care, which refers to care, diligence, skills, and judgment "expected of any auditor in similar circumstances." It also means maintaining confidentiality between the audit team members and the client and not disclosing information to any third parties "without the expressed approval of the client and, where appropriate, the approval of the auditee unless required by law."

Systematic Procedures

Audits are flexible management tools but their use should enhance consistency and reliability. The exact procedures for any audit will differ somewhat depending upon the type of company, its business, and its culture. The standard recognizes this but emphasizes that whatever the exact nature of the audit, it should be conducted "according to documented and well-defined methodologies and systematic procedures." For any type of environmental audit, the methods and procedures should be consistent.

EMS AUDIT PROCEDURES—ISO/DIS 14011

ISO/DIS 14011 transforms the general principles of ISO 14010 into specific, generic procedures for auditing environmental management systems. It's important to emphasize that the standard focuses on auditing environmental management systems. These refer to systems for planning, control, and review of *operations.* System audits have been distinguished from auditing for compliance with laws, regulations, and other requirements. This type of auditing evaluates the *environmental performance* of the organization's operations against criteria such as regulations (i.e., Does the level of emissions of a substance exceed legally allowable levels?).[3]

In the case of ISO 14011/1, the audit process focuses on determining the existence and proper functioning of the management system elements, not whether specific performance complies with legal or other requirements. The major steps in the process begin on page 101.

ISO/DIS 14011/1—Guidelines for Environmental Auditing—Audit Procedures—Part 1: Auditing of Environmental Management Systems

Table of Contents

Determine the Audit Scope and Objectives

The EMS audit should have a clearly defined scope, determined by the lead auditor and the client and normally including consultation with the auditee. The scope describes the extent of the audit and sets its boundaries (i.e., which site(s), which activities, how the results are reported). Any subsequent changes to the audit scope must be agreed to by the client and lead auditor.

The audit should also be based on defined objectives. Although the primary objective is to determine EMS conformance to EMS criteria, ISO/ DIS 14011/1 lists some other typical objectives:

- To determine whether the EMS has been properly implemented and maintained.
- To identify areas for potential improvement of the EMS.
- To assess the capability of the internal management review process to ensure the continuing suitability and effectiveness of the EMS.
- To evaluate the EMS as part of a potential contractual relationship.

Assign Roles and Responsibilities

The size and makeup of the audit team will vary with the scope and objectives of the audit. ISO 14011 describes the roles of the lead auditor, auditor, audit team, client, and auditee. The lead auditor is responsible for ensuring the efficient and effective performance of the audit according to the plan approved by the client. The lead auditor, in consultation with the audit team members, assigns team members to specific EMS elements, functions, or activities to audit. During the audit, the lead auditor can change the work assignments if necessary to achieve the audit objectives.

Review Preliminary Documents

The lead auditor reviews existing documentation, such as the organization's environmental policy statements, programs, records, manuals, and all appropriate background information on the auditee's organization. If the auditor judges the documentation to be inadequate, he or she informs the client, and the auditors should not expend additional resources until they receive further instructions from the client.

Prepare the Audit

Preparation involves designing a comprehensive, yet flexible audit plan. (See Box.) The plan is communicated to the client, auditors, and auditee. It is then reviewed and approved by the client. If the auditee objects to any provisions of the plan, the objections are communicated to the lead auditor. The lead auditor, the auditee, and the client resolve the issues and agree to a revised audit plan before or during execution of the audit.

The audit team members are given specific EMS elements, functions, or activities to audit and instructions on the procedures to follow. Then they gather working documents to facilitate the audit. These can include forms, checklists, procedures, and records of meetings. The standard notes the importance of maintaining these working documents until the completion of the audit and of safeguarding confidential or proprietary information.

The Audit Plan

ISO/DIS 14011/1 notes that the audit plan should include the following items, where applicable:

- Date and locations of audit.
- Audit team members.
- Expected time and duration of major audit activities.
- Schedule of management meetings.
- Audit objectives, scope, and criteria.
- The organizational and functional units to be audited.
- Functions and/or individuals in the organization with significant direct responsibilities regarding the auditee's EMS.
- Identification of the EMS aspects that are of high audit priority.
- Procedures for auditing the EMS as appropriate to the organization.
- Working and reporting languages of the audit.
- Reference documents.
- Confidentiality requirements.
- Report content, format and structure, date of issue, and distribution of reports.
- Document retention requirements.

Execute the Audit

The standard details the key steps: conduct an opening meeting; collect evidence; record audit findings; and hold a closing meeting. The key here is to use consistent, reliable procedures.

Opening Meeting

The audit typically begins with an opening meeting whose purpose is to:

- Introduce the audit team to the auditee's management.
- Establish the official communication links between the audit team and the auditee.
- Review the audit scope, objectives, and plan and agree on an audit timetable.
- Summarize the audit methods and procedures to be used.
- Confirm that the necessary resources and facilities are available.
- Confirm time and date for the closing meeting.
- Promote active participation by the auditee.
- Review site safety and emergency procedures for the audit team.

Collecting Audit Evidence

Next, the auditors collect audit evidence through interviews, examination of documents, and observation of activities and conditions. There should be sufficient audit evidence to support audit findings that the EMS conforms to the EMS audit criteria. The auditors record indications of nonconformity.

Information gathered through interviews should be verified by supporting information from independent sources, such as observations, records, and results of existing measurements. Auditors should identify nonverifiable statements as such.

Auditors should also examine the basis of relevant sampling programs and the procedures for ensuring effective quality control of these processes.

Audit Findings

The auditors record all significant audit findings and review them to determine where the EMS does not conform to the audit criteria. The nonconformities are documented clearly and supported by evidence. The findings should be reviewed with the responsible auditee manager to obtain acknowledgment of the factual basis of the nonconformity findings.

In a note, ISO 14011/1 adds that if it is within the agreed scope of the audit, the auditors can also document findings of conformity, but should exercise due care to avoid any implication of absolute assurance.

Closing Meeting

After the evidence has been collected but before preparing the audit report, the auditors meet with the auditee's management and those responsible for the functions audited. The auditors present audit findings to the auditee so that the auditee can clearly understand the findings and acknowledge their factual basis.

Disagreements should be resolved before the lead auditor issues the report. Final decisions concerning the significance and description of the findings ultimately rest with the lead auditor, though the auditee or client can still disagree with these findings.

Audit Reports and Records

The final major step is to prepare and distribute an accurate, complete, and written audit report. The lead auditor works with the client to determine what goes in the report and is responsible for its preparation, accuracy, and completeness. The lead auditor signs and dates the report.

The report can include but is not limited to the following information:

- Organization audited and the client commissioning the audit.
- Organization's representatives participating in the audit and the audit team members.
- Audit period and date(s) it was performed.
- Audit objectives and scope.
- Criteria against which the audit was conducted, including a list of reference documents against which the audit was conducted.
- A summary of the audit process, including any obstacles encountered.
- Audit findings or a summary of them, with reference to supporting evidence.
- Audit conclusions (if requested by client).

- A statement of the confidential nature of the contents and the distribution list for the audit report.

Audit conclusions, according to ISO/DIS 14011, can include:

- Whether the EMS conforms to the EMS audit criteria.
- Whether the system is properly implemented and maintained.
- Whether the internal management review process is able to ensure the continuing suitability and effectiveness of the EMS.

Corrective action. A note to the ISO 14010 standard emphasizes that it's the responsibility of the client or auditee to determine if corrective action(s) are needed to respond to the findings. The auditor, however, "may provide recommendations when there has been a prior agreement to do so with the client."

Report Distribution

The lead auditor sends the report to the client within the agreed timetable. The client determines how the report should be distributed, according to the audit plan. The auditee should receive a copy unless specifically excluded by the client. Additional distribution of the report outside the auditee's organization requires the auditee's permission.

A key issue is confidentiality and disclosure. Audit reports are the sole property of the client and it's up to the auditors to safeguard confidentiality. There is no requirement in the standards to disclose any information to third parties. Any distribution outside the organization requires the permission of the organization being audited. It's also important to note that there is no requirement for communicating audit results to third parties.

Document Retention

All working documents, drafts, and final reports pertaining to the audit should be retained by agreement between the client, lead auditor, and auditee and in accordance with any additional requirements. In keeping with confidentiality, auditors may not disclose any documents without the express permission of the client and the auditee.

ISO 14012 QUALIFICATION CRITERIA FOR ENVIRONMENTAL AUDITORS

The third standard in the series details qualifications for environmental auditors. ISO/CD 14012 applies to both internal and external auditors and can also be used to accredit auditors. It applies to the selection of auditors to perform audits as described in ISO 14010 and ISO 14011/1.

The standard notes that internal auditors should be as competent as external auditors. But the standard leaves room for flexibility, especially for smaller companies. Internal auditors might not meet all the criteria, depending on two factors:

- The size, nature, complexity, and environmental impacts of the organization.
- The rate at which internal auditors develop relevant expertise and experience.

Individual Auditors, Not Teams

The standard applies to individual auditors, not to the criteria for the selection and composition of audit teams; this is described in ISO/DIS 14011/1.

DEFINITIONS

ISO 14012 adds a few definitions to the auditing series. An *environmental auditor* is a "person qualified to perform environmental audits." Due to differences in educational systems around the world, the standard also defines degree and secondary education as follows:

A *degree* is a "recognized national or international degree, or equivalent qualification, normally obtained, after secondary education, through a minimum of three years formal full time, or equivalent part time study." *Secondary education* is "that part of the national educational system that comes after the primary or elementary stage, but that is completed immediately prior to entrance to a university or similar establishment."

Key Qualifications

The standard focuses on the need for auditors that have the following experience and qualifications.[4]

Education and work experience. Auditors should have some combination of education and work experience, either a secondary education or equivalent and five years of work experience or a degree and a minimum of four years of appropriate work experience. In both cases, the standard allows for a reduction of the work experience by a year or two by satisfactory completion of formal post-secondary full time or part time education.

The work experience of auditors should contribute to developing skill and understanding in some or all of the following areas:

- Environmental science and technology.
- Technical and environmental aspects of facility operations.
- Relevant requirements of environmental laws, regulations, and related documents.
- Environmental management systems and standards.
- Audit procedures, processes and techniques.

Formal and on-the-job training. The standard also calls for both formal and on-the-job training, provided either by the auditor's own organization or by an external organization. The requirements for formal training address the areas described above. The criterion for formal training may be waived in some or all of the areas if the auditor can demonstrate competence through accredited examinations or relevant professional qualifications.

On-the-job training should total 20 equivalent work-days of environmental auditing and a minimum of four environmental audits. This should include involvement in the entire audit process under the supervision and guidance of the lead auditor and should occur within a period of not more than three consecutive years.

Personal attributes and skills. The standard recognizes that education and knowledge is not enough for effective auditing. In addition to the above skills, auditors should possess personal attributes and skills that include the following:

- Competence in clearly expressing concepts and ideas, both orally and in writing.
- Good interpersonal skills, such as diplomacy, tact, and the ability to listen.

- The ability to maintain independence and objectivity.
- Personal organizational skills needed for efficient auditing.
- The ability to reach sound judgments based on objective evidence.
- The ability to react with sensitivity to the conventions and cultures of the country or region in which the audit is performed.

Due professional care. The auditor should exercise due professional care and should adhere to an appropriate code of ethics.

Language. The final clause of the standard emphasizes that audit team members should not participate unsupported in audits if they can't communicate effectively in the language necessary. When necessary, they should get the support of a person with necessary language skills, but one who is not subject to pressures that would affect the performance of the audit.

Maintenance of competence. The standard emphasizes that auditors should maintain competence to make sure their knowledge of the areas described above is complete and should participate in refresher training, if necessary.

Lead auditor. The lead auditor should be capable of ensuring effective and efficient management and leadership of the audit process and must meet the following additional criteria:

- Demonstrate capability by means of interviews, observation, references, and/or assessments of auditing performance made under quality assurance programs

or

- Participate in the audit process for a total of 15 additional equivalent work-days, for a minimum of three additional complete audits

and

- Participate as acting lead auditor for at least one of the above three audits.

The lead auditor should meet the additional criteria within a period of three consecutive years.

Annexes

ISO 14012 includes two short informative annexes. *Annex A* provides guidance for evaluating the qualifications of environmental auditors. This can be an internal or external evaluation process. The Annex lists some methods for evaluating auditor candidates, including:

- Interviews.
- Written and/or oral assessment.
- Review of candidates' written work.
- Discussions with former employees and colleagues.
- Role playing and peer observation under actual audit conditions.
- Review of records of education, training, and experience.
- Consideration of professional certifications and qualifications.

Annex B addresses very briefly the issue of developing a body to ensure a consistent approach to the registration of environmental auditors. It points out that the body may register auditors directly or accredit other organizations who in turn register the auditors. The body should establish an evaluation process subject to a quality assurance program and keep a register of auditors who meet the criteria specified in ISO 14012.

Environmental Site Assessments

WG4 of Subcommittee 2 is developing a proposal for a standard on environmental site assessments. WG4 must prepare a justification for moving ahead with a standard four months prior to the June 1996 meeting of TC 207. The proposed standard could focus on legal liability only or become a comprehensive guideline that covers all relevant environmental matters pertaining to a due diligence investigation in preparation for acquisition or divestiture. In either case, the goal of the assessment is to collect information to determine whether there are any adverse environmental aspects of the site that can affect its value or legal liability.

According to the proposal, a rationale in favor of the standard is that more companies are doing business on a global scale, including buying and selling properties and businesses abroad. Site assessment standards would be a useful tool to encourage consistency in the scope and level of environmental site assessments. An argument against the proposal is that national and regional legal liabilities and regulatory requirements are so localized that developing a useful international site assessment standard may not be practical.

PRACTICAL CHALLENGES IN AUDITING AN EMS

The ISO 14001 standard is a generic management standard. It does not contain specific performance requirements and focuses on the "what" not the "how" of environmental management. The ISO 14010–12 standards are also general, baseline standards. There are concerns among standards developers and auditors that EMS auditing is distinct from auditing for compliance or performance and that the ISO 14011 auditing standard doesn't provide sufficient guidance for auditing to ISO 14001. The possible consequence? Inconsistent interpretation of the standards and loss of confidence in the resulting ISO 14001 certificates.

For example, although ISO 14001 specifies in general what the environmental policy must address, specific policies depend on several factors, such as the company's business sector, the kinds of environmental issues it must face, the nature of its internal culture, and other such issues. According to audit managers, EMS auditors must be able to evaluate the adequacy of a specific environmental policy in the context of the company's particular situation.

Thus, the auditing process inevitably becomes somewhat subjective. As one auditor put it, a compliance question usually has a yes or no answer, but a management system question can be answered in several ways.[5] According to many auditors, this inherent subjectivity raises the need for extensive experience in environmental issues as well as familiarity with management systems.

Management Systems versus Environmental Experience

A key issue for auditing to ISO 14001 will be to find the right balance in auditor skills between environmental knowledge and general management systems knowledge. Auditors with extensive experience in environmental issues may focus on the details of environmental performance while overlooking or not recognizing system problems.

On the other hand, auditors with primarily management systems experience may not have the experience to evaluate the EMS and how it deals with issues such as significant environmental aspects. Early experience from auditing to the UK's BS 7750 standard indicate that teams composed of auditors with varying skills may be most effective approach.

EMS Audit Protocol

A task group in the United States is working on developing an EMS auditing protocol document that offers auditors guidance in auditing an environmental management system. The group is looking at each element in the ISO 14001 EMS specification and identifying how to evaluate whether the specific EMS element required is in place and possible sources of information to assist the auditor in making the determination.

According to members of the group, the Annex doesn't necessarily add detail to the auditing standard but clarifies the kinds of questions auditors should ask and what to look for. For example, to assess whether the environmental policy is appropriate to the nature, scale, and environmental impacts of the organization's activities, the auditor will review the statements in the policy statement, examine documents that detail the nature and scale of organization's activities, and interview operations and environmental staff to gain insight into the environmental impacts of the activities. To determine whether the environmental policy "is available to the public," the auditor might look for the existence of a procedure for public communication and evidence such as public announcements, publication of the policy in annual reports, inclusion in company newsletters, on a company Internet site, and so on.

CONCLUSION

Information gained from environmental auditing is critical to developing, maintaining, and improving an environmental management system program. Internal audits must be of high quality to provide useful information for making business decisions that have not only financial but also social and political implications.

Regarding third-party registration audits, early auditing experience with EMS standards such as BS 7750 and the EMAS regulation indicates that consistent and effective auditing is critical to the ultimate acceptance of the ISO 14000 standards and the development of a credible conformity assessment system worldwide. The ISO 14010–12 standards lay a foundation for achieving these goals. There remain several issues to resolve, however. A few of these include:

- How do auditors interpret generic requirements such as "environmental aspects" and "significant environmental impacts"?

- Will auditors be compelled to report noncompliances to authorities?
- How will auditors tread the fine line between determining the existence of required EMS elements and judging the actual environmental performance achieved by the organization?

These practical challenges and others await the actual implementation of ISO 14001 and the experience gathered by EMS auditors.

NOTES

1. Environmental Auditing Policy Statement, EPA, Final Policy Statement, Federal Register 51, no. 131, Wednesday, July 9, 1986, p. 25004.

2. This has been an ongoing source of debate during the drafting process. To what degree does the EMS auditor judge the effectiveness of the EMS in actually meeting its objectives? Can an EMS audit be successful unless the auditor evaluates performance? These issues remain open for debate and will be resolved only through experience in EMS auditing.

3. From *Types of environmental audit and associated ISO activities—A discussion document.* ISO/TC 207/SC 2 N76, 4/10/95.

4. Some delegations to TC 207 believe that the existing standard focuses too much on determining qualifications through time spent in school and in work experience. They recommend more of a focus on determining actual competencies through alternative methods. SC2 will consider these arguments in any future revision process of ISO 14012.

5. Telephone interview with Dawne Schomer, Corporate ESH Audit Program Manager, Texas Instruments, Inc., May 1995.

Chapter Seven

Environmental Performance Evaluation

The ISO 14001 standard calls on companies to develop specific, measurable objectives and targets. The standard also requires them to evaluate the performance of their EMS and to improve it. Environmental performance evaluation (EPE) is a tool to achieve these goals, and Subcommittee 4 is developing standards that any organization can use to monitor how it's doing.

Why is measurement in the form of environmental performance evaluation important? The basic idea is that if you can't measure performance, you can't really improve it. If you don't know where you are now, you won't know where you're going or whether or not you got there. Measurement sets the framework for management, in the sense that a company can only effectively manage what it measures. Measurement turns vague, general goals into specific targets that everyone in the company can understand and support.

The goal of EPE is to give management a useful tool for generating the accurate information it needs to measure and track environmental performance to help meet its objectives and targets. The EPE process covers the full life cycle of the company's products and services, from raw material input through production and disposal. At its heart is the selection of environmental performance indicators (EPIs) that give the organization its key yardsticks with which to evaluate progress.

Compared to auditing, which has achieved some level of acceptance, EPE is a relatively new area with important implications for companies. Not only does EPE assist the organization to monitor how it's doing; it also helps the organization communicate its performance, both internally to employees and externally to all stakeholders. EPE is thus a critical tool for environmental management. Thus, the work of SC4 is garnering increasing interest of delegates to TC 207 and organizations outside the ISO process.

SCOPE OF SC4'S WORK

The scope of SC4's work is defined by SC4 as "standardization in the field of environmental performance evaluation for use by organizations to measure, assess, and communicate their environmental performance for appropriate management purposes." SC4 has two working groups. The goal of both groups is to contribute to developing a generic standard for environmental performance evaluation. The standard will guide organizations to measure, evaluate, and describe environmental performance and to communicate information about performance to management and other interested parties. It is designed to promote the use of EPE by all organizations as an integral part of their environmental management system.

The developing standard is intended to be useful to organizations whether or not they have or plan to develop a formal environmental management system that complies with ISO 14001. It will be useful for any size or type of organization. An important caveat: the standard is for guidance only. It's not for use as a specification standard for registration purposes.

The Status of Subcommittee's Work

The standard that forms the basis for the discussion in this chapter is at the working document stage, *ISO/WD 14031 Evaluation of the environmental performance of the management system and its relationship to the environment.* This standard is being revised and the first committee draft (CD) is planned for mid-1996. Several annexes to ISO/WD 14031 are also in development by various task groups. A DIS is not expected in this area until 1998 after the CD is used for pilot testing. Since ISO/WD 14031 is under development and will likely change, the description that follows explains the key concepts and issues being debated by SC4 but is not a literal description of every detail in the standard nor the exact flow of the contents. The discussion is supplemented by material from other documents submitted to SC4 and from deliberations that have taken place during the drafting process.

Key terms and definitions. The proposed standard incorporates definitions from ISO 14001 and adds a few additional ones. (Keep in mind that as the standard develops, these definitions may be slightly altered.)

Environmental performance. Environmental performance consists of the "measurable results of an organization's management of the environmental aspects of its activities, products and services." A note adds that in the context of environmental management systems, the results "may be measured against the organization's policy, objectives and targets."

Environmental performance evaluation (EPE). Environmental performance evaluation is a process to "measure, analyze, assess, and describe an organization's environmental performance against agreed criteria for appropriate management purposes."

Environmental performance indicator (EPI). An EPI is a "specific description of EP within an evaluation area."

EPE IS NOT EMS

There are some key phrases in these definitions. One is "appropriate management purposes." The EPE standard is generally not used to directly establish goals, objectives, and targets separate from the environmental management system. Environmental policies, objectives, and targets are set by management as part of the EMS process.[1] Environmental performance evaluation, however, is a useful tool that can generate valuable information which management can then use to set specific, measurable goals and objectives.

ISO/TC 207 recognizes, however, that the EPE standard may be used as a stand-alone document. It may be used by organizations that either do not have an EMS system in place yet or do not plan to develop one. For such organizations, the process can generate information for setting goals, objectives, and targets.

EPE information helps the company prioritize its environmental aspects and significant impacts. It provides valuable, ongoing input to the various stages of the EMS process, including planning, implementation, monitoring, measurement, and management review.

The EPE standard does not contain any performance requirements. There are no targets for companies to meet.

ISO 14001 VERSUS ISO 14031

The ISO 14001 standard, in Clause 4.4.1, calls on a company to "monitor and measure on a regular basis the key characteristics of its operations and activities . . . This shall include the recording of information to track performance, relevant operational controls, and conformance with the organization's objectives and targets." Basically, the EPE process described in ISO/WD 14031 helps companies do this.

Note too that ISO 14001 doesn't reference ISO 14031 because the EPE standard is a guidance, not a specification or conformance standard. Therefore, to comply with ISO 14001, an organization need not follow the exact process described in ISO 14031. Nor would the organization have to set up an elaborate EPE management process that's separate from the EMS. In short, ISO 14031 is not an extension of ISO 14001.

EPE VERSUS EMS AUDITING

The EPE process is also distinct from environmental auditing and the ISO environmental auditing standards. EPE is a continuous process of collecting and analyzing ongoing information.

This distinguishes it from EMS auditing, which is an occasional activity. Both EMS auditing and EPE are EMS tools. The purpose of EMS auditing, however, is to confirm that an organization's EMS system is in place and achieving its goals. The purpose of EPE is to generate useful information to measure performance results against objectives and targets. Auditing is a "verification activity while EPE is a measurement activity."[2]

Is EPE an internal measurement tool or system to publicly compare companies? Part of the EPE process is to communicate information about environmental performance. This information can be used by external parties to compare the environmental performance of companies. This is of particular interest to nongovernmental environmental organizations. Such organizations want to have confidence that the environmental performance of ISO 14001 companies is good. External communication of EPE information is part of the EPE process, but the primary use of EPE is for internal management purposes.

BENEFITS OF EPE

The EPE process has several benefits. Measuring performance over time can provide insight into problem areas and opportunities for improvement. It can help manage every element of the EMS process. It can set the stage for root-cause analysis and problem solving. EPE can create a basis for pollution prevention, better allocation of resources, and better regulatory compliance.

EPE can help organizations evaluate environmental risks and plan for preventing potential problems. It can provide financial information for cost-benefit analysis. It is important information for the management review process described in ISO 14001 in that it looks at the suitability and effectiveness of the EMS itself.

If the organization is setting up an EMS, it can help it pinpoint strengths and weaknesses and identify environmental aspects and significant environmental impacts.

GENERAL OVERVIEW OF EPE

The EPE process has four basic elements:

- Planning the EPE process:
  Reviewing environmental aspects.
  Setting the scope of the EPE process.
  Collecting information.
  Selecting and validating environmental performance indicators.
- Applying the EPE process:
  Collecting and analyzing data.
  Evaluating environmental performance.
- Describing environmental performance:
  Communicating and reporting for internal and external purposes.
- Reviewing and improving the EPE process.

PLANNING THE EPE PROCESS

Planning involves reviewing or identifying environmental aspects of the organization's activities, products, or services. The environmental aspects are compatible with the EMS policies, objectives, and targets. The standard suggests that the time to plan for EPE is during the development and setting of the environmental objectives and targets.

If no formal EMS is in place, the review establishes an overview of the organization's environmental issues and identifies significant environmental aspects. The basic purpose is to identify what the organization wants to measure.

Environmental Performance Indicators (EPIs)

Critical to the EPE process is selecting appropriate environmental performance indicators. As mentioned above, an EPI is defined as a "specific description of environmental performance within an evaluation area."

For example, an EPI for water usage could be the "percent reduction in net consumption usage of water." A material-usage EPI could be "volume of materials used per unit of output." An EPI for personnel training could be the "hours of training per employee" or the "resources spent on training per employee." Other examples of EPIs include the following:

- Number of toxic release incidents over time.
- Number of incidents investigated with determination of root causes.
- Percent reduction in transportation energy.
- Air emissions in kg/unit of production.
- Discharges of effluents in kg/unit of production.
- Hazardous waste generated in kg.
- Weight of packaging per consumer product.
- Amount of CO_2 released to atmosphere.

The definition and selection of EPIs is a relatively new process and lies at the heart of EPE. An important rationale for pilot-testing the CD of the environmental performance evaluation standard is to develop useful and practical sector-specific EPIs.

An Analytical Tool for Selecting EPIs

To help sort out the myriad of potential measurement areas, the ISO 14031 working document describes an analytical classification tool for evaluating and selecting appropriate environmental performance indicators: the management system, the operational system, and the state of the environment.[3]

Management System

The management system includes people, procedures, and activities throughout the organization involved in planning, controlling, and verifying environmental performance. The management system receives inputs from laws, regulations, the operational system, interested parties, and the state of the environment. Evaluating the management system can yield, among others, EPIs that describe the strengths or weaknesses of the organization and can help identify root causes of nonconformance.

Operational System

The operational system includes the design and operation of the plants and equipment that generate the products, processes, and/or services. It also encompasses the flow of mass and energy that is required to produce the products or services. The operational system also encompasses linkages among activities, plants, and sites. Both the management system and the operational system are under the control of the organization.

State of the Environment

The organization doesn't exist in a vacuum, but is a part of the environment. Its management and operational activities occur in the context of the environment and impact the state of the environment. Thus, an EPE system also incorporates ways to describe and measure the environmental impacts of the organization's activities. These impacts can be local, regional, or global.

They can include impacts in the following areas:

- *Land use* (such as impacts on wetlands, on desertification and erosion, or increased loss of nutrients from the soil).
- *Biological diversity* (such as acidification of water and resulting fish deaths).
- *Ecological* (such as global climate conditions, evidenced by changes in precipitation, higher global temperature, etc.).
- *Human health* (such as toxicological impacts).[4]

The primary use of the state-of-the-environment classification is as a context for selecting specific indicators that measure the impacts on the environment from the organization's activities, products, and services.

The process of evaluating and measuring environmental impacts, however, is complex, and correlations are difficult to identify.

With local conditions, it may be possible to isolate the organization's impact on the environment or at least to identify a reasonable correlation. For example, if a plant is the only one discharging a substance into a local body of water, it may be possible to measure, over time, changes in the fish population, the degree of acidification of the water, and so on. Over time, this information may be useful to management in making decisions about emissions to the body of water.

However, making correlations between the plant's activities and its impacts on global, regional, or even local conditions is complicated. For example, the operational system might measure the amount of CO_2 released by the plant. The state of the environment measurement could be the amount of CO_2 in the air within the vicinity of the plant. Developing some cause-and-effect relationship between these two indicators is possible, but difficult. The amount of CO_2 in the air within the vicinity of the plant could be caused by several factors other than the amount released by the plant itself.

Linkages between the Management and Operational System

The management and operational system are linked. The evaluation of environmental performance is facilitated when an issue is traced from the management through the operational system. For example, the management system can set a target for decreased emissions; the operational system monitors the amount of emissions per unit of production and takes into consideration the impact on the environment—the amount of emissions actually released into the air.

Defining the Scope of the EPE Process

It's important to define the scope of the EPE process. The scope varies depending on the nature of the organization and its structure. It varies depending on the environmental policy and the environmental issues the organization must address. It's up to management to decide where to apply EPE, including which operating units, facilities, products, or services, and how broad the scope will be, that is, whether it will include the supply and distribution of goods, services, and energy and extend to waste disposal and the activities of suppliers.

Collecting Information for EPE Planning

The EPE planning process requires information to be collected from a variety of sources. These include the organization's objectives and targets, its management needs, the requirements and expectations of interested parties, and existing environmental performance information.

Identifying, Validating, and Selecting EPIs

Planning culminates in identifying potential EPIs within the management and operational systems, assessing their validity, and selecting the appropriate ones for the organization. The ISO 14031 working document describes several ways to characterize EPIs (see Box.)

The document points out that the organization should select EPIs that are as simple and understandable as possible. It should also try to strike a useful balance between too many EPIs that can complicate the EPE system and too few EPIs which may not provide sufficient information to management.

Ways to Characterize EPIs

There are several ways to categorize EPIs, including the following:

Absolute. An absolute EPI refers to basic data without analysis or interpretation. For example, the total emissions of SO_2.

Relative. A relative EPI compares the data to another parameter. For example, SO_2 emissions per ton of primary product.

Indexes. An indexed EPI would result from constructing a baseline year at 100 percent or weighing of equivalents to consolidate data, such as total greenhouse gas releases expressed as CO_2.

Aggregated. This refers to collecting data for a number of related factors either vertically or horizontally in the organization, such as SO_2 emissions aggregated from 20 plants. Aggregation is useful in making huge amounts of information useful for decision making. Data can be aggregated by combining it from various sites over time, or by assigning data to a category of environmental effect. For example, the amount of hazardous waste generated per site.

Weighted. This involves weighting of noncomparable effects. This is a political process and consists of value judgments.

Validating EPIs

Are the potential EPIs that the organization is considering valid? The EPE process includes evaluating EPIs to determine how useful they are for EPE purposes. Invalid EPIs can lead to inundating management with masses of irrelevant information. The proposed standard offers several criteria to validate EPIs (see Box).

Criteria to Validate EPIs

The standard suggests the following criteria to validate EPIs.

Scientifically valid. The EPI should be technically sound; that is, verifiable, reproducible, and comparable.

Representative. The data that the EPI conveys should represent the condition of the problem/issue in general.

Responsive to change. A useful EPI shows trend changes within a reasonably short time.

Predictive. The EPI should provide early warning of future trends that it purports to measure.

Target/threshold for comparison. The EPI should be capable of being compared to a target so that users can assess its significance.

Cost effective. The EPI should be cost effective, in terms of obtaining and using the data, compared to its value.

Data adequacy/availability. The data used to develop the EPI should be accurate and available in a timely manner. The measuring and monitoring system should be reliable.

Relevant and understandable. The EPI should be relevant to the organization's objectives and the needs of decision makers. It should also be simple and clear and understandable by nonspecialists.

Selecting EPIs

A primary goal of the EPE process is to select EPIs relevant to the organization's strategy and objectives. The EPIs should be linked to the organization's objectives. The organization should select EPIs for both the management and operational systems. The working document offers some considerations in selecting the appropriate EPIs, including the following:

- Select EPIs that are simple, understandable, and the minimum number to provide the necessary information.
- Select quantitative EPIs for physical processes and operations.
- Select financial measures to estimate cost savings and the impact of environmental initiatives on the organization.
- Use qualitative EPIs when quantitative ones aren't feasible.

APPLYING THE EPE PROCESS

The next basic aspect of the EPE process is application. According to the proposed standard, applying EPE involves four basic steps: collecting and analyzing data, then aggregating and assessing information.

Collecting Data

The key point is to collect data in a systematic way that ensures its quality and validity. Much of the data for EPE may already be available, including data from regulatory reporting, emission rates, risk management information, financial, or inventory operations. It's important to determine the minimum frequency at which data should be collected to meet its intended use.

Data quality will require quality assurance and control procedures to make sure the results are credible. The process should provide for collection, filing, storage, maintenance, retrieval, and disposition of the information to maintain the relevance of the results.

Verifying the accuracy of the data is another important part of the process. Records for verification purposes include inspection reports, test data, compliance records, and calibration reports. The procedures must also ensure the validity of sampling protocols, data collection methods, and modeling techniques.

Analyzing Data

Analyzing data involves taking the raw data and transforming it into useful indicators so it can be used to compare actual performance with objectives and targets. For example, the raw data can be the amount of SO_2. The associated EPI could be SO_2 per product generated. The analysis can be expressed in quantitative, qualitative, or relative terms.

The working document emphasizes that the analysis should be unbiased and that it should include all relevant information, even if it doesn't support the organization's view of its performance.

Aggregating Information

It is often useful to aggregate data. The proposed standard cautions against combining unlike elements and recommends the recognition of scientific uncertainty. Releases to different media (air, water, land) are usually not grouped together unless they impact the same area. For example, sulfur dioxide air releases and sulfuric acid releases should not be aggregated unless both affect the level of acidity of the same water body. Also, an organization with multiple sites generally would not aggregate the releases of toxic materials because they affect different local communities.

Evaluating Environmental Performance

The final step is to evaluate the EPIs and compare them to the organization's objectives, its information needs, and the expectations of interested parties. If there are problems, the evaluation can focus on root-cause analysis, corrective action, and plans for improvement. The EPE process also provides information for revising objectives and targets.

DESCRIBING ENVIRONMENTAL PERFORMANCE

The next major element of the EPE process is describing environmental performance. The organization should plan for internal and external communication. A communication plan demonstrates management commitment to environmental protection. It increases awareness of the organization's objectives and reduces concerns about environmental issues.

Internal Communication

Types of environmental performance information that can be reported internally include:

- Compliance information.
- Potential legal and financial liabilities.
- Current status of the organization's environmental performance.
- Opportunities for improvement.
- Expectations of interested parties.

External Communication

External communication is directed to interested parties such as local community groups, environmental organizations, stockholders, insurers, suppliers, and customers. Of course, it will include regulatory bodies.

The standard notes that communication to external parties should be based on the organization's needs. A few factors might include whether the organization:

- Has a stated environmental policy on external communication.
- Believes external communication will improve its business position and its relations with interested parties.
- Subscribes to a voluntary initiative (such as EMAS) that requires external communication.
- Receives significant requests for information related to its environmental performance.
- Publishes an environmental report.

Regarding this last item, EPIs can form the basis for the information presented in a company's environmental report. For example, an Environment, Health, and Safety Progress Report published by Xerox lists, among others, the information based on the following EPIs:

- Pounds of releases of chemicals to publicly owned treatment works.
- Percent of solid waste recycled.
- Percent of total hazardous waste shipped off-site for recycling/ reuse.

Effective external communication results when an organization clearly understands its target audience, the information it needs to provide, and what it hopes to achieve by providing the information.

REVIEWING AND IMPROVING THE EPE PROCESS

As with any management process, it's important to review and improve the EPE process. Review and improvement are the final aspects of the overall system.

The basic EPE process is fluid. An organization can start simply, by focusing on a few key EPIs that it can directly affect and influence. Then, as its control of environmental issues increases and it begins to integrate the EPE process into its overall EMS, it can develop the process to encompass additional EPIs. The organization can then identify new environmental issues, develop more effective EPIs, and find better and more accurate data collection methods.

The EPE process supports continual improvement of the EMS by providing progress information about environmental performance. This helps management set new objectives and targets. And, in turn, the better the organization can understand its environmental performance, the better it can refine the EPE process itself.

The EPE process and proposed standard will give any organization the critical management tool it needs to achieve its objectives and goals. To conclude by ending the same way we began, the axiom holds: If you can measure it, you can improve it. And the better you can measure performance, the more you can improve it.

NOTES

1. SC4 is debating the use of the phrase "decision makers" versus "management." There is general agreement in SC4 that either term can be used throughout the organization, both vertically and horizontally.

2. From comments made by Chris Bell, an attorney from the Sidley & Austin law firm and US delegate to TC 207, during working group meetings of the US SubTAG to SC4.

3. There is a proposal to change the concept of evaluation areas to encompass two basic areas: the management system and the operational system. The state of the environment area is viewed, not as another evaluation area per se, but as the context for identifying and selecting various environmental performance indicators for the management and operational systems. Although the standard is in development, the discussion in this chapter is based on this proposal.

4. A group in SC4 is considering a menu of indicators for sustainable development. The indicators are presented in a Driving Force-State-Response framework. "Driving Force" indicators indicate human activities, processes, and patterns that impact on sustainable development; for example, a driving force indicator for protecting human health could be the "percentage of infants without access to safe drinking water." "State Indicators" indicate the "state" of sustainable development associated with the driving force; for example, "the infant mortality rate." "Response Indicators" indicate policy options and other responses to changes in the state of sustainable development. In our example, this may be the "percent of GDP spent on health."

P A R T

III

ENVIRONMENTAL MANAGEMENT
Product and Process Evaluation

Internal Organization for Standardization
Technical Committee 207

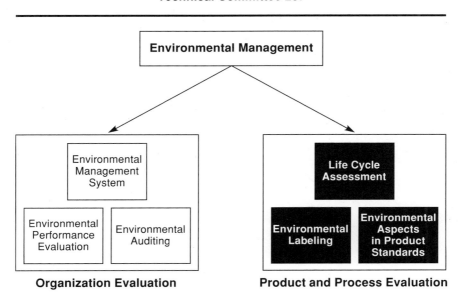

Chapter Eight

Life Cycle Assessment

The previous chapters of this book focused on setting up an environmental management system and evaluating it using tools such as environmental auditing and environmental performance evaluation.

Another series of standards in the ISO 14000 family focuses not on the system per se but on the characteristics of products, processes, and services. Primary among these standards are environmental labeling and life cycle assessment (LCA). LCA is the subject of this chapter.

More companies are taking a closer look at the entire life cycle of their products, from raw materials through production to distribution, possible reuse, and disposal. They are examining the effects of their operations, both direct and indirect. The direct effect of paper recycling would be less disposal and less solid waste. An indirect effect of recycling, however, is that it requires energy to run the recycling operation.[1]

Companies increasingly use the life cycle concept to help them make better business and environmental decisions.[2] Life cycle assessment is one approach among others that include design for the environment and industrial ecology. Both of these approaches aim to take into account all environmental aspects of industrial operations for the purpose of increasing efficiency, improving the bottom line, and protecting the environment. (See Box.)

Design for the Environment and Industrial Ecology

Life cycle assessment is one approach among several to better understand the interaction between industrial activity and our environment. *Design for the Environment* (DfE) encompasses efforts to design products and processes in ways that can eliminate or minimize the creation of pollution. DfE can lower the cost of hazardous waste disposal and reduce the expenses

(Continued)

(Continued)

associated with regulatory compliance. Part of the DfE process is to encourage businesses to understand the full range of environmental costs and to integrate these into basic business decision-making. Among the methods under development in this area are environmental accounting and capital budgeting. The term *full cost accounting* or *total cost accounting* refers to accounting methods that allocate environmental costs, both direct and indirect, to a product, product line, process, service, or activity. These methods help decision makers to measure and quantify the benefits of pollution prevention in the design of products and processes.

Industrial ecology is a broad system concept based on a general analogy with natural ecological systems. Industrial ecology is the study of how materials and energy flow and are transformed within broad industrial and consumer activities, the kinds of effects that these flows have on the environment, and the influence of a variety of factors on the system. These factors can be economical, political, societal, or regulatory. Industrial ecology seeks to place such systems within the framework of regional and global issues such as acid rain, ozone depletion, global climate changes, and other such developments. The goal is to make more environmentally sound decisions regarding the operation of industrial systems.

WHAT IS LIFE CYCLE ASSESSMENT?

Before defining the word *assessment,* a broader term would be *life cycle thinking* or the *life cycle perspective.* Basically, life cycle thinking means taking a holistic environmental view of a product or service, from raw materials through production to distribution and final disposal. This perspective encourages companies to look at all environmental aspects of their operations and helps them integrate environmental issues into their overall decision-making process.

Even if an organization does not conduct an actual life cycle assessment, the life cycle perspective can be useful especially if it is introduced to people in the company who wouldn't otherwise be as aware of the environmental aspects of their tasks, such as the purchasing department.

Life cycle assessment is the methodology that applies the life cycle perspective. It is the analysis of a product or service system throughout all stages of the life cycle: raw materials acquisition, manufacturing, transportation, use/reuse/maintenance, recycling/waste management, and the relevant energy supply systems.

There are several frameworks for LCA methodology in current use. The one that forms the basis for the work of TC 207's Subcommittee 5 has been developed by the Society of Environmental Toxicology and Chemistry (SETAC). This approach has several phases, including the following.

First, it involves defining the goals and scope of the assessment.

Second, it involves measuring the materials and energy used and environmental releases that arise along the entire continuum of the product or process life cycle. This continuum encompasses the extraction and processing of raw materials, manufacturing, transportation and distribution, use/reuse/maintenance, recycling, and final disposal. Inputs include energy and raw materials. Outputs include water effluents, airborne emissions, solid waste, and other environmental releases. This process is known as a *life cycle inventory analysis.*

Third, the information obtained from the inventory analysis is used to examine the impact on the environment. This is known as *life cycle impact assessment.* It examines the actual and potential environmental and human health effects associated with the use of resources such as energy and materials and with the environmental releases that result. The inventory analysis stage doesn't directly assess the environmental impacts of the inputs and outputs. It provides the information for the impact assessment. The impact assessment then converts the data from the inventory analysis into descriptions of the environmental impact.

Finally, the information from the impact assessment is used to systematically evaluate and implement opportunities to make environmental improvements based on the knowledge gained from analyzing environmental impacts. The goal is to identify those parts of the system that may be changed in order to reduce the overall burden or impact of the product or service system. This process is known as *life cycle improvement assessment.*

This process, although theoretically ideal, has not often been used in the real world. Until now, most LCA studies haven't gone beyond the life cycle inventory analysis phase of quantifying resource and energy use and releases.

Part of the reason is that the LCA methodology is not well developed. Another reason is that a more limited analysis is often valuable in its own right. Sometimes it's possible to perform an analysis of a system without including all of the life cycle stages (to focus only on alternative raw material usages, for example).

APPLICATIONS AND BENEFITS OF LCA

Reduce Environmental Releases and Manage Risks

An LCA can help a company identify opportunities to reduce emissions, and energy and material use. Using a life cycle inventory analysis, a company can establish a baseline of information on its plant's resource and energy use and identify opportunities for improvement. It can make decisions about the best suppliers to use and whether to substitute raw materials to cut down on resource use.

LCA is also a risk management tool that helps companies understand the environmental risks throughout the product/process life cycle. If the company has developed an environmental performance evaluation program, the LCA process can improve the precision and accuracy of environmental performance indicators.

Guide Product Development

LCA can be useful in product development, planning, and design. Companies are moving beyond focusing only on waste generation and energy use and are looking at factors related to product design. An LCA analysis can help a company identify the stages in the product life cycle where the greatest impacts occur. In some cases, it is possible to correlate specific raw material use, energy use, and waste emissions to specific products in a plant to discover how the product lines contribute to the overall resource use.

Plays a Role in Labeling

A product life cycle assessment process plays an important role in labeling programs that involve environmental claims and also in marketing products. Some form of LCA is used in many of the over two dozen national labeling programs in operation today. The role of LCA in labeling and environmental claims is discussed in the next chapter.

Public-Sector Applications

LCA can be used by the public sector, not only in connection with environmental claims but also in developing public policy measures. For example, according to the EPA in the United States, it may consider LCA as a tool to implement the Executive Order on "green procurement" and other initiatives. Germany may use LCA information as a basis for taxing packaging. Nongovernmental organizations can use LCA information to make policy recommendations.

LCA'S LIMITATIONS

The LCA tool also has limitations. LCA studies are time and resource intensive. Data gathering is complex and expensive. Data quality can be poor. The methodology has not been standardized. Conceptually, only the goal definition/scoping and the life cycle inventory analysis stages of the overall LCA process are reasonably well established and defined. Impact assessment and improvement assessment are conceptually defined methods but are not well developed or documented.

The processes that LCA attempts to analyze are very complex. LCA methods involve many varieties and sources of data. The data varies in availability. In any organization, it's not always possible to collect all the data. Therefore, LCA isn't a purely scientific process. It involves making assumptions, value judgments, and trade-offs. For example, recycling involves trade-offs since energy is required to transport materials to the recycler and for reprocessing into useful material. This also requires energy and results in emissions and solid waste.

Cause-and-effect relationships in the impact assessment process are hard to pinpoint. Although the inputs and outputs to any industrial system can be measured or estimated, the causal link between these factors and environmental impacts is not always clear. Thus, the results of the impact assessment are partly subjective. Comparative judgments sometimes resemble the "apples and oranges" comparison. For example, is global warming more important than ozone depletion?

Making projections on the basis of LCA information can also be questionable. For example, the results of an LCA focused on local issues often are not appropriate in a regional or global application and vice versa. If the study uses data that has been aggregated from many sources, it can overlook local variations in energy use and pollution generation.

Claims based on LCA studies, especially comparative claims, or comparative assertions, are especially tricky. They may be misleading or ill founded. People unfamiliar with LCA may wrongly assume they are being informed about the total environmental impact of the product or wrongly assume one product is better than another.

And LCA is not the only tool available. To fully explore its environmental aspects and impacts, a company can also benefit from risk assessment and environmental auditing.

Development of Life Cycle Assessment

Although life cycle assessment has been the subject of growing interest only within the past few years, it has actually been practiced, mostly limited to the life cycle inventory assessment, since the late 60s and early 70s. In 1969, the Coca Cola Company funded studies to compare the environmental impacts of different types of beverage containers. LCA studies were conducted in the 1970s focusing primarily on energy use, given the context of concern with energy shortages.

Interest in LCAs waned in the late 70s and early 80s but then increased for many of the reasons already discussed in this book: increased concern with the environmental impacts of industry, serious environmental accidents, the impetus for companies to become more efficient by looking at a broader range of issues, from "cradle to grave."

Governments began to look at LCA as well. In the mid-80s, the European Commission issued a directive on food containers that called for companies to monitor the energy and raw materials consumption and solid waste generated by their products. LCA was a tool for performing such an analysis. In 1992, the European Union launched its Eco-label program. This labeling program uses life cycle concepts as part of its objectives and in the methods for selecting product criteria. (See the next chapter for an explanation of environmental labeling.)

In 1990 and 1992, the Society of Environmental Toxicology and Chemistry (SETAC) organized workshops that brought LCA practitioners together. The result of these workshops is a conceptual and methodological framework for LCA that is referenced in the draft ISO LCA standards.

PURPOSE AND SCOPE OF SC5

Turning now to SC5 on life cycle assessment, its published scope is standardization in the field of life cycle assessment as a tool for environmental management of product and service systems.

The subcommittee has two general tasks and five working groups. The first task, that of WG1, is to develop a standard on general principles and guidelines of life cycle assessment. This is *ISO/CD 14040 Environmental*

Management—Life cycle assessment—Principles and guidelines. This standard provides an overview of the LCA process and establishes general guidelines, principles, and procedures for initiating, conducting, and reporting life cycle assessment studies in a responsible and consistent manner.

The second task is to develop specific standards for the inventory analysis, impact assessment, and improvement assessment phases. The first of these standards—*ISO/WD 14041 Environmental management— Life cycle assessment—Goal definition/scope and inventory analysis*—is being developed by WG2 and WG3. The ISO/WD 14041 working document explains how to define the goals and scope of an LCA study and the general method for conducting an inventory analysis.

WG4 is developing a standard for impact assessment, and WG5 was originally assigned the task of developing a standard on life cycle improvement analysis. This last stage of the LCA process, however, is now viewed by the standards developers as an application of LCA, not part of the basic methodology, and is now considered the Interpretation Phase.

Life Cycle Assessment Standards in Development

WG1. *ISO/CD 14040 Environmental management—Life cycle assessment— Principles and guidelines.*

WG2&3.* *ISO/WD ISO 14041 Environmental management—Life cycle assessment—Goal definition/scope and inventory analysis.*

WG4. ISO 14042 Life cycle assessment—Impact assessment (in development).

WG5. 14043 LCA Life cycle assessment—Improvement assessment (or evaluation and interpretation).[†]

* These two work groups have been combined.

[†] The actual titles of this and the other standards may change during the development process.

Guidance, Not Registration

Among the goals of SC5 are to develop useful and flexible LCA tools that describe a consistent methodology and create a common understanding of LCA. Another goal is to provide methods for reporting LCA studies in a responsible, transparent, and consistent manner.

The draft standards are designed not only for LCA practitioners but also for environmental managers and others in organizations who are unfamiliar with LCA and want to understand what it is and how to use it.

As with all of the draft standards in the ISO 14000 series, except for ISO 14001, the LCA draft standards provide guidance; they do not contain specifications for registration or certification purposes. Other draft standards in the ISO 14000 series refer to life cycle assessment, but there is no requirement in ISO 14001 to perform life cycle assessment according to ISO/CD 14040 or any other requirements.

Products, Services, and Processes

Although most LCAs up to this point have focused on product systems, the methods and the standards take into account services and processes. Application of LCA to services and processes is increasing. Sectors in Europe are applying LCA to the electrical generation industry and to transportation.

ISO/CD 14040 AND ISO/WD 14041—SYNOPSIS

The following is a synopsis of the key concepts in both the ISO/CD 14040 and ISO/WD 14041 draft standards. Keep in mind that the documents are in development and are likely to change; the discussion, therefore, focuses on those key concepts that, at least according to the judgment of the authors, will remain in future drafts of the standards. ISO/CD 14040 is an overview of the life cycle assessment methodology. ISO/WD 14041 focuses on two phases of the methodology outlined in ISO/CD 14040: goal definition/scope and inventory analysis.

Key Points

One useful tool among several. The introductions to the standards emphasize that life cycle assessment is one useful tool among several to help companies better understand, control, and reduce environmental impacts created by goods and services. These impacts include resource depletion, human health, and ecological consequences.

Not limited to third-party use. The LCA standards are not limited to application by third-party practitioners but are also for internal use. The intent of the draft standards is to encourage public policy makers, private organizations, and the public to approach environmental issues in a systematic manner that takes into account the environmental impact of a broader range of activities than has traditionally been the case.

Recognize the limitations. The draft standards emphasize the limitations discussed earlier in this chapter. It cautions organizations to clearly communicate assumptions, to avoid unsubstantiated claims, and to be very cautious when making environmental claims based on LCA results, especially comparative claims. LCA results should not be reduced to simplistic solutions but should clearly communicate the complexities involved.

Not designed to freeze evolution. The draft standards also emphasize that their purpose is not to freeze the evolution of LCA methods; the methods should be applied flexibly to reflect developments in the field. Organizations can apply the core elements of LCA in the way most practical and appropriate for their needs.

Improve consistency and technical validity of LCAs. The purpose of the standards is not to describe the "perfect LCA study" and then require organizations to conform to these ideals of perfection. Instead, it is to improve the consistency and technical validity of LCAs that are performed so that the LCA methodology develops with some measure of worldwide credibility.

Limited studies. The Introduction to the ISO/WD 14041 draft standard notes that partial or "streamlined" LCA studies can also be necessary and useful. These may not encompass the entire product service life cycle. For example, a study might focus only on developing databases for raw materials or energy supply systems. Or it may deal only with site-specific effects, such as worker safety or risk assessment. Wherever possible, such studies should follow the requirements of the standard.

A few key definitions included in the standard are shown in the adjoining box.

Selected Definitions in ISO/CD 14040

Environmental impact. Consequences for human health, for the well-being of flora and fauna, or for the future availability of natural resources, attributable to the input and output streams of a system.

Life cycle. Consecutive and inter-linked stages of a product or service system, from the extraction of natural resources to the final disposal.

Inventory analysis. Phase of LCA involving the compilation and quantification of inputs and outputs for a given product or service system throughout its life cycle.

Impact assessment. Phase of LCA aimed at understanding and evaluating the magnitude and significance of environmental impacts based on the life cycle inventory analysis.

Life cycle assessment. Systematic set of procedures for compiling and examining the inputs and outputs of materials and energy and the associated environmental impacts directly attributable to the functioning of a product or service system throughout its life cycle.

OVERVIEW OF THE LCA METHODOLOGY

This section outlines the essential elements of LCA methodology described in the ISO/CD 14040 standard and the ISO/WD 14041 working document.

DEFINING THE GOALS AND SCOPE OF AN LCA

The first step in any LCA is to clearly understand its goals and scope. The goals of an LCA should be clearly defined and encompass:

- Why the study is being performed.
- Who's sponsoring the study.
- The participants in the study.
- How the organization intends to apply the study and use the results.
- The intended audience.

- The initial quality of data required for the LCA.
- The type of critical review to be employed.
- Requirements for communicating the results of the LCA.
- Limitations on the use of the study for other purposes.
- The sponsors and participants in the study.

The goals of a study may vary. It could be to establish some baseline conditions for a system so that a company can identify and evaluate the most significant inputs and outputs. Or it could be to lay the basis for a comparative claim.

The scope of the study should be defined well enough, in terms of its breadth and depth of analysis, to achieve the stated goals of the LCA. The scope should include:

- The function(s) of the system.
- The functional unit.
- The system(s) to be studied.
- The boundaries of the system.
- Data requirements.
- Assumptions and limitations.

The ISO/WD 14041 working document notes that as LCA data is collected in a study, the scope may be modified and even the goals of the study itself revised due to unforeseen limitations or constraints.

Function and Functional Unit

The LCA study should clearly define the function of the system it's going to study. The *function* of a paint company would be to provide paint. The function of a soft drink manufacturer would be to provide soft drinks to customers. The function of a grocery bag process is to provide means for customers to carry groceries. The *functional unit,* however, is the measure of performance that the product or service system delivers. That is, what measurable, specific result does the system produce?

The functional unit for a paint system could be the "unit surface area covered" if the function is to deliver protective and decorative covering to a wood surface. The ISO/WD 14041 working document notes that if the function is changed to include durability, the functional unit could be "unit surface protected for defined period of time."

In comparative studies it is important to compare products or service systems whose functions are equivalent. The ISO/WD 14041 working document gives an example: If the function of the system is to produce one kg of polyethylene, it cannot be compared to a system whose function is to produce one kg of polypropylene.

Another example of equivalent function and use would be in comparing cloth diapers to disposable diapers. One type of diaper may typically be changed more frequently than the other, and market/use studies show that often cloth diapers are doubled, whereas disposable ones are not. Therefore, the functional unit for purposes of comparison would be the "total number of diapers used over a set period of time."

Systems and Subsystems

The ISO/WD 14041 working document notes that although industry is concerned primarily with *products,* LCA focuses on *production systems.* A system is any collection of operations that, when acting together, perform some defined function (see Figure 8–1).

FIGURE 8–1
Life Cycle Assessment Process

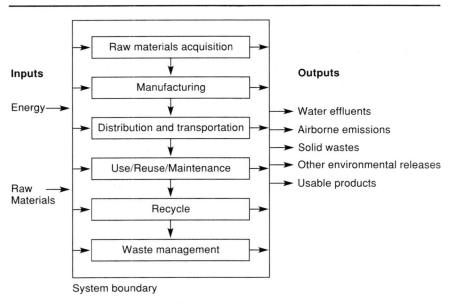

Within each system are separate *subsystems* or *unit processes*. It's necessary to break down a complex system into unit processes such that each unit process is a single operation for which the organization can actually gather input and output data. It's important to define where each unit process or subsystem begins, in terms of raw or intermediate materials, what happens during the process, and where it ends, in terms of the intermediate or final product.

The physical description of the system is a quantitative description of all flows of material and energy—inputs and outputs—across the system boundary. The ISO/WD 14041 working document emphasizes that it's critical to define the system specifically.

System Boundaries

The system boundary separates the system from its surroundings—the system environment. The environment provides inputs into the system and receives all outputs from the system. Part of the scoping process is to define what's not in the system. For example, the extraction of raw materials may not be defined as part of the system, so that there will be no inventory of energy and resource uses during the extraction process.

A system boundary can be a physical boundary, such as all operations performed by a particular piece of machinery. Or it can extend beyond a single, physical operation; for example, the organization may analyze its transportation operation, which extends beyond a specific location.

The system boundary helps the organization decide where to limit its analysis. For example, the boundary for the raw material element of the inventory begins with all activities necessary for the acquisition of a raw material or energy and ends at the first manufacturing or processing stage that refines the raw material.[3] The boundaries of the use/reuse/maintenance system begin after distribution of finished products or materials to an end user takes place and end at the point at which those products or materials are discarded and enter a waste management system.[4]

The ideal study would trace all energy and material inputs back to their original extraction from the earth. Similarly, it would trace all releases to their ultimate destination. But this is usually impractical, so the organization must decide where and how to cut off the analysis. That's why defining the system boundary is so important.

A good LCA study clearly states the criteria for setting the system boundaries. One criterion could be whether the specific life cycle stage is not significant; that is, a stage could be excluded if the inputs and outputs associated with it are not significant enough, compared to the overall system.

Other considerations emphasized by the working documents include the intended application, assumptions made, and the intended audience.

Defining Inputs and Outputs

Once the systems, subsystems, and boundaries are defined, the systems are outlined using a flow process diagram to show the relationship between the unit processes. The main reason to analyze the system and its component unit processes is to produce a listing of the inputs and outputs to each unit process. These are the flow of materials and/or energy from one unit operation to another.

Data Categories and Data Quality Requirements

Data categories classify the types of inputs and outputs that cross the system boundaries. Inputs include raw materials and energy. Outputs include waste heat, solid waste, air emissions, water emissions, and usable products.

LCA studies generate huge amounts of data. It's important to define the goals for data quality to ensure the study is credible. Data quality goals specify in general terms the desirable characteristics of the necessary data. These depend on the objectives and application of the study. For example, a study focusing on a specific company at a specific site will emphasize obtaining recent, site-specific data, while a public study will emphasize independently verified data.

When the data will be used to make comparisons, the standard calls for LCA studies to assess the precision, completeness, and representativeness of the data and to assess the consistency and reproducibility of the data collection and calculation methods used throughout the LCA.

THE LIFE CYCLE INVENTORY ANALYSIS

After the goal and scope of the study are clearly defined, the next phase of the LCA methodology is the inventory analysis.

Data Collection

The main task of the inventory analysis is to collect data to measure the flow of the inputs and outputs of energy and materials associated with the system. Data collection is a complex and resource-intensive process, and the procedures will vary with the scope, the system, and the intended application of the LCA. The ISO/WD 14041 draft document calls for the study to model the system using flow charts, describe each unit process in detail, list the data categories from which data is desired, define the units of measurement, and describe sampling techniques.

Finalizing the system boundaries. During the data collection process (if not before), the system boundaries are often finalized based on some cut-off criterion that limits the subsequent data handling. An example of a cut-off criterion might be values for data that are below a certain threshold.

Calculation

Calculation procedures are necessary to generate the inventory of results for a specific functional unit and the defined system. The working documents describe several steps in the operation:

- Prepare the data and make calculations within each subsystem.
- Analyze the data to identify problems, gaps, inconsistencies, or data that is nondetectable.
- Aggregate data from different sources, if necessary, for communication between the LCA practitioner and the user or for external purposes.
- Connect the subsystems to allow calculations of the complete system.
- Relate functional units of each system when comparing products or service systems.

The standard notes that each of these operations may introduce additional uncertainty to the original data, which should be kept in mind when judging the validity and representativeness of the overall results.

LIFE CYCLE IMPACT ASSESSMENT

The proposed ISO/CD 14040 standard describes life cycle impact assessment in general terms. The purpose of life cycle impact assessment is to understand and evaluate the magnitude and significance of environmental impacts based on the inventory analysis. The methodology of impact assessment is complex and still in development. The ISO/WD 14041 working document presents three steps in the process: classification, characterization, and valuation.

Classification is grouping and sorting the data from the life cycle inventory into a number of impact categories. The general categories are resource depletion, human health, and ecological impacts. Under these general categories, the organization can define specific categories (such as global warming or water acidification under the ecological category).

Characterization is analyzing and quantifying the impact in each selected category. An important component is the use of relevant physical, chemical, biological, and toxicological data that describe the potential impacts.

The working document notes that characterization based on inventory data is not a measure of actual environmental impacts. Current approaches attempt to model or to represent potential, possibly uncertain, impacts.

The final step in impact assessment is a discussion of the relative significance of its results. **Valuation** may involve interpretation, weighting, and ranking of the data from the inventory analysis. Of course, some of this necessarily involves value judgments (for example, Is global warming worse than ozone depletion?).

Conclusion and Interpretation

The conclusions of the LCA answer the questions posed in the goal definition. Conclusions can be presented at the end of either the inventory phase or the impact assessment phase. The basic goal is to organize the results of the LCA into comprehensible, meaningful information for decision makers.

REPORTING

The results of an LCA should be fairly and accurately reported to the intended audience, whether internal or external. The information in the report should contain enough detail to allow the reader to understand, interpret, and use the results in a manner consistent with the goals of the study. The goal is to make the methods and the data transparent to the audience.

SC5 is debating the issue of additional reporting requirements needed for LCAs that are used for comparative assertions, and whose results are reported to third parties. Comparative assertions are claims released to the public regarding the superiority of one product versus a competing product. The primary rationale would be to hold such LCAs to a slightly higher standard to reduce the misuse of LCA results when making such comparative assertions.

CRITICAL REVIEW

A critical review is an independent examination of the LCA study to determine its validity and credibility. The critical review is important because LCA practice won't evolve without credible LCA studies.

Also, when the ISO LCA standards are adopted worldwide, there will be value attached to those LCA studies that claim to fulfill the requirements of the ISO LCA standards. (Remember, however, these standards are for guidance purposes only, not for verification or certification purposes by third parties. There is no plan at this time to set up third-party registration systems to verify conformance with the ISO LCA standards under development.)

The critical review answers key questions about the study:

- Were scientific and technically valid methods used, given the goal of the study?
- Was reasonable and appropriate data used?
- Are the conclusions valid, given the goal?
- Is the study transparent and consistent?

The ISO/CD 14040 draft standard emphasizes that critical reviews are optional but recommended, especially when the organization performing the LCA study uses it to make comparative assertions that are disclosed to the public.

The scope of a critical review is established through mutual agreement between the organization conducting the LCA and those performing the critical review. It should be clear why the review is being undertaken, what will be covered, to what level of detail, who should be involved in the process, and what data must be made confidential.

The standard describes four levels of critical review: self review, expert or practitioner review, peer review, and stakeholder review.

Self Review

The person(s) conducting the LCA can perform the critical review. This person(s) can be assisted by an internal expert. The review statement is prepared by the person conducting the LCA study and is included in the LCA study report.

Expert or Practitioner Reviews

In this situation, the review statement is also prepared by the person conducting the LCA study. It can then be reviewed by an external independent expert or LCA practitioner. Another option is to have the review statement prepared by the expert or practitioner, not by the person conducting the LCA. The review statement, comments of the expert, and any response to recommendations made by the reviewer are included in the LCA study report.

Peer and Stakeholder Reviews

In these situations, an external independent practitioner is selected to act as chair of a peer review panel. Based on the goal, scope, and budget available for the review, the chair selects other reviewers with appropriate experience and expertise to conduct the review.

The committee can include stakeholders that will be affected by the results of the LCA study, such as industry competitors, government agencies, advocacy groups, scientific organizations, consumer groups, environmental organizations, and trade unions. Here, too, the review statements would be included in the LCA study report.

Conclusion

The LCA standards are a bit like the starship *Enterprise* in "Star Trek." They are going places in standardization no one has gone before. Although expert practitioners are developing increasingly sophisticated LCA methods, the LCA effort—unlike most ISO standards work—isn't standardizing well-accepted and well-understood methods and procedures. There are also wide disparities in awareness and understanding of LCA methods worldwide.

As the drafting process continues to develop, there will be key issues to resolve. A few of these include the following.

Marketing Tool

LCA is purported to be scientific but can easily be misused. It is difficult if not impossible to measure all the environmental risks of products. Using LCA as a marketing tool in product claims or in labeling is a major concern and will remain a concern until the methodology develops farther and is based on sound scientific techniques. The purpose of standardization is to promote this development.

Apples and Oranges

As mentioned earlier, the apples-versus-oranges problem will continue, as will the issue of making trade-offs. Take the familiar cloth-versus-disposable diaper argument. Cloth diapers use about 60 percent more water and create a greater volume of water pollution than disposables. But disposables generate more than seven times as much trash and use more energy. What's more important, conserving water or minimizing trash? In an area where water is at a premium, the decision may favor disposables. Where landfills are hard to find, cloth might be better.

Trade Problems

As will be discussed in the next chapter, trade problems can result from the use of life cycle assessment in labeling programs. It can occur if government regulations, based on life cycle results, discriminate against imported products. Discrimination deliberately intended to block imports and protect domestic industries is illegal under the international trade rules of the General Agreement on Tariffs and Trade (GATT). These trade issues and the possible trade barriers resulting from LCA use are of special concern to many developing countries.

Practicality

Significant factors for many companies are practicality and costs. Full-blown LCA studies can be very expensive. In certain situations, limited or "streamlined" studies designed for internal purposes can be valuable. It's possible to use life cycle concepts to make improvements at many stages of a product or service process. Companies can substitute raw materials; find better uses for waste; change the style, type, or amount of packaging; and make many other improvements as a result of applying the life cycle concept.

CONCLUSION

In summary, the interest in life cycle assessment reflects a concern with the impact of industrial activities on the environment. More companies are looking at the use of LCA to make their operations more efficient and place fewer burdens on the environment. If the LCA standards are useful and the LCA methods are adopted worldwide, they will assist companies in achieving these goals.

NOTES

1. From *Life Cycle Analysis Methodology,* presented at an Environmental Issues Conference, May 2, 1991, by Jere D. Sellers, Robert G. Hunt, et al.

2. A recent survey conducted by Tufts University in the United States indicated that, of the 34 Fortune 500 companies (primarily based in North America) that were known to be involved in LCA, 22 are actively using LCA, 6 are at the pilot stage, and 4 are planning to use LCA in the near future. From Thomas Gloria, Theodore Saad, Magalie Breville, and Michael O'Connell, "Life-Cycle Assessment: A Survey of Current Implementation," *Total Quality Environmental Management,* Spring 1995, pp. 33–50.

3. Society of Environmental Toxicology and Chemistry, *A Technical Framework for Life-Cycle Assessment,* Workshop Report (SETAC Foundation, 1990), p. 9.

4. Ibid., p. 59.

Chapter Nine

Environmental Labeling

In recent years, the public has become more concerned about the negative impacts of products and services on the environment. The 1980s and early 1990s saw increasing news coverage of environmental problems, from disasters such as Exxon *Valdez* to potential global problems such as acid rain, global climate change, and ozone depletion.

As consumers, many in the public have taken the initiative to try to lessen these potentially negative impacts by purchasing products that they perceive are less harmful to the environment than similar other products.

Manufacturers, in turn, have responded to consumer demands by making and advertising claims regarding the environmental attributes of their products. Many are also introducing so-called green products or redesigning existing products to make them less harmful to the environment.

In many cases, these claims appear as labels on the products and/or packaging. To gain credibility for their claims, manufacturers have submitted products to third-party labeling programs. Countries around the world have instituted labeling programs that award such labels. Germany began in 1978, Canada and Japan in 1988. By now, over two dozen such programs are in place.

These programs vary in methods and approaches. The need for an international, reliable standard to harmonize national labeling programs and offer guidance to manufacturers who want to make environmental claims has given rise to the work of Subcommittee 3 of TC 207 on labeling.

BASIC PURPOSE OF LABELING

Labeling has several purposes. One is to provide clear and accurate information for consumers, so that they can make informed buying decisions. A broader policy purpose goes to improving the environmental performance of industrial operations. One way to do this is to harness the marketplace in favor of environmental protection.

Labeling programs that award labels to manufacturers of products that cause less harm to the environment are intended to encourage other companies to follow suit and improve their products to gain the label and the resulting increase in market share.

Harmonize Existing Programs

Different rules and procedures for labeling and making environmental claims create complexity and potential trade barriers. Labeling programs can lead to trade barriers by favoring products within the nation that is operating the program. This creates potential obstacles for other producers trying to enter the marketplace.

The goal of harmonization is to reduce the complexity and overlap by use of standards. Note, we said harmonize, not homogenize. The aim of the ISO work is not to make all labeling programs the same but to achieve some consistency in methods and procedures.

Voluntary adherence to the proposed ISO labeling standards would result in:

- Claims being determined on the same basis.
- Labels awarded on the basis of similar procedures.

The ISO labeling work is designed to set technically valid framework criteria against which the existing programs can be measured. The result? Labeling programs that conform to the standards will have more credibility in the global marketplace to the extent they follow ISO guidelines.

SCOPE OF SUBCOMMITTEE 3

The scope of SC3 is broad. It goes beyond labeling per se and covers environmental claims of any type. This includes environmental reports, such as "green annual reports," advertising, and marketing communications. The subcommittee is divided into three working groups.

WG1—Practitioner Programs

Working Group 1 is developing a guidance standard that describes principles and practices of third-party multiple-criteria labeling programs. This is *ISO/CD 14024 Environmental labeling—Practitioner programs—Guiding principles, practices, and certification procedures of multiple criteria programs.* This standard is undergoing revision and will be reissued as a CD for ballot in early 1996.

Third-party, multiple-criteria programs typically look at a product's environmental attributes and award a single label that represents an overall judgment about the product's environmental attributes. Almost all the over two dozen programs operating worldwide are of this type.

The ISO labeling standards will not replace existing programs but instead will complement them by providing internationally accepted methods, criteria, and procedures for operating such programs and making environmental claims.

The exception to the multiple-criteria, single-label approach is the program that does not award a single label but instead supplies an environmental profile of a company. An example is the Environmental Report Card awarded by Scientific Certification Systems in the United States. The Environmental Report Card does not certify that a product has certain superior environmental attributes as compared to other products in its class. It simply conveys information about the environmental attributes of the product in quantitative or qualitative fashion without preset selection criteria or selection of superior products. This approach is generally similar to nutritional labeling, which doesn't tell you which food is better in a class. A New Work Item proposal for a standard regarding this type of labeling is being prepared for consideration by TC 207.

WG2—Self-Declaration Claims

Self-declaration claims are those made by a manufacturer that address specific aspects of a product, such as whether it is recyclable, biodegradable, and so on. Working Group 2 is developing three standards. The first is *ISO/CD 14021 Environmental labeling—Self-declaration environmental claims—Terms and definitions.* This standard (discussed below) presents common definitions for key claims made by manufacturers. The second standard will focus on the use of symbols in environmental claims, such as the familiar recycling loop. The third standard will deal with methods for testing and verifying self-declaration claims.

WG3—Principles of all Environmental Labeling

Working Group 3 is developing a guidance standard that describes key principles applicable to all types of environmental labeling. This is *ISO/ CD 14020 Principles of all environmental labeling.*

POTENTIAL IMPACT OF THE LABELING STANDARDS

Improve Performance

A key anticipated impact of the standardization effort will be better environmental performance and reduced environmental burdens. The degree to which this goal should be made explicit in the standard is still under debate. Few, however, debate that the ultimate impact of standardization should benefit the environment.

De Facto Requirements

Although the standards are formally voluntary, they could become standard industry practice or be adopted by government regulators as guidelines. That is, the standards could become de facto requirements. Retailers, contractors, even consumers could expect or demand that environmental claims comply with ISO standards. Environmental groups and other nongovernmental organizations could use the standards as yardsticks against which to judge labeling programs.

Improve Claims

Hopefully, one impact of the standards effort will be to improve claims. Manufacturers making self-declaration claims will have a better idea of what's a legitimate claim. They will be less prone to making loose or irresponsible claims. The standards will provide common global definitions for key terms, such as recyclable, biodegradable, and so on.

Defend Products against Trade Barriers

Invoking the standards may be useful in defending the product interests of a country, since the standards contain language that warns against the use of labeling programs as potential trade barriers.

PRINCIPLES OF ALL ENVIRONMENTAL LABELING

We discuss the work of WG3 first because its proposed standard lays out key guiding principles for the development and use of environmental labels. The following is a summary of the ISO/CD 14020 standard.

Remember that the standard is still under development and the following might change in future revisions.

Introduction

The introduction to the standard re-emphasizes the important role that the ISO 14000 series standards can play in improving environmental performance worldwide. The ISO 14020 guidelines are part of the EMS series and, although the labeling standards can be used independently, they are tools for the EMS.

What Do Environmental Labels Do?

Environmental labels provide information about a product or service in terms of its overall environmental character, a specific environmental attribute, or any number of attributes. Purchasers can use this information in choosing the products or services they desire, based on environmental as well as other considerations.

The introduction notes that product or service providers expect that the environmental label/declaration will influence the purchasing decision in favor of their products or services. If this happens, the market share of such products or services increases and other providers may respond by improving the environmental attributes of their products or services to enable them to also make such claims. Thus, the use of environmental labels/declarations, based on accurate, nondeceptive, and verifiable information stimulates the potential for "market-driven continuous environmental improvement."

Definitions in ISO/CD 14020

Environmental label/declaration. This is a claim that indicates the "environmental attributes of a product and service that may take the form of statements, symbols, or graphics on product or package labels, product literature, technical bulletins, advertising, publicity, etc."

Purchaser. The purchaser is "anyone in a product or service supply chain who buys the product or service from a seller."

Life cycle. Life cycle refers to "consecutive and inter-linked stage of a product or service system, from the extraction of natural resources to the final disposal."

KEY PRINCIPLES

Environmental labels should be accurate, verifiable, relevant and nondeceptive. If a label does not provide accurate information about the environmental aspects of a product, it won't be effective. The factual and technical basis for the labeling claim must be verifiable. The label should provide relevant, not trivial information about environmental attributes. It should be understandable and not misleading to the average intended consumer.

The standard emphasizes that programs should periodically review the basis for awarding the labels and gather information at an appropriate frequency to keep up with the pace of innovation.

The party that makes the label/declaration should make the relevant information about environmental attributes available to purchasers. Purchasers can't make informed choices until they fully understand the meaning of the claim, symbol, or term. This can be achieved by advertising, explanatory information at the retail level, education programs, and other methods.

Environmental labeling should be based on thorough and comprehensive scientific methods that produce accurate and reproducible results. For a claim to be credible, it must be based on scientific methods that are widely accepted and recognized. Where appropriate and possible, such methods should follow recognized standards such as those of ISO. Or they could follow industry/trade methods that have been subjected to peer review. The methods used should be appropriate to the claim being made and should provide relevant and necessary information.

Information concerning the process and methodology used in environmental labeling shall be available to all interested parties. To be credible, a labeling program's process and methods must be transparent. Users and other stakeholders need sufficient information about underlying principles, assumptions, and boundary conditions to be able to evaluate and compare labeling programs and to assess whether the claim is consistent with applicable standards in the ISO 14000 series.

Environmental labeling should, wherever appropriate, incorporate the life cycle of the product or service. The life cycle concept allows the party making the label/declaration to take into account a range of factors that impact the environment. The standard therefore recommends a life cycle approach to assist in identifying appropriate and relevant characteristics and/or criteria for the label. The life cycle concept can also be used to determine the significance of a claim.

Administrative and information requirements should be limited to those necessary to establish conformance with applicable criteria and/or standards of the labels/declarations. In other words, participation by interested companies, both large and small, in labeling programs shouldn't be hindered by unnecessary costs, administrative complexity, or unreasonable administrative demands.

Environmental labeling should not create unfair trade restrictions or discriminate in its treatment of domestic and foreign products and services. This principle addresses the all-important issue of potential trade barriers posed by labeling programs. The standard gives some examples:

- Requirements to meet specific national or local legislation, regulations, or standards rather than performance objectives.
- Restrictions on testing methods such as:

  Requiring national or local procedures rather than internationally accepted methods.

  Restrictions on the recognition of testing facilities that result in creating impossible geographic requirements.

  Inequitable application of costs, fees, charges, or requirements.

  Administrative requirements that limit access by foreign producers to the program or limit their ability to comment on the development of criteria.

Another potential trade barrier is created by the simple lack of flexibility in the program to take into account environmental conditions that may be different in foreign countries. These different conditions can create obstacles for products from those countries that are being submitted to the labeling program of the importing country.

The standard notes that these issues lie within the sphere of international trade rules such as GATT and states that additional language explaining the trade issues will be included in future revisions. (WG3 has established a task group to provide input on the trade barrier issues.)

Environmental labeling should not inhibit innovation that maintains or can potentially improve environmental performance. A labeling program, by awarding a label, shouldn't freeze technological innovation. Requirements should be expressed in terms of performance rather than design or descriptive characteristics to avoid discouraging improvements in products or services that could lead to significant environmental improvement.

Standards and criteria applicable to environmental labels should be developed through a consensus process. The process for developing standards and criteria should be open to all interested parties. This can be encouraged by timely and adequate notification. Labeling programs should be responsive to comments and other submitted input.

ISO/CD 14024 ENVIRONMENTAL LABELING— PRACTITIONER PROGRAMS—GUIDING PRINCIPLES, PRACTICES, AND CERTIFICATION PROCEDURES OF MULTIPLE-CRITERIA PROGRAMS

The ISO/CD 14024 draft standard contains guidance for multiple-criteria programs, and it addresses procedures and methods used by labeling programs worldwide. The standard is under development and has been the subject of much debate concerning its objectives, content, level of pre-scriptiveness, detail, and other aspects. There is considerable debate, for example, about the trade implications of labeling and the adequacy of the way this is addressed in the proposed standard. Thus, the following description is meant not to be comprehensive but primarily to give the reader a sense of the direction in which this standard is moving, not its specific destination.

What Is a Multiple-Criteria–Based, Third-Party Labeling Program?

The introduction to ISO/CD 14024 defines a third-party, multiple-criteria–based labeling program as the use of labels to inform customers that a third party has certified that the labeled product meets a set of predetermined criteria. These criteria were chosen to "promote environmentally sound purchasing decisions for products of that category." The resulting label asserts the preferability of the product based on a multiple-criteria–based assessment of equivalent products or services.

Such programs are voluntary and the labels are awarded by either government sponsored or private organizations. The standard emphasizes that labeling programs cannot be involved in the manufacturing, distribution, or sale of the product or service for which the label is awarded.

Labeling Is Not Product Certification

The ISO/CD 14024 draft standard emphasizes that a label indicates that the product meets the criteria of the labeling program. It does not mean that the product has been certified to product standards. For products to be sold in certain markets, they must meet a variety of product certification and regulatory requirements. These are distinct from the labeling criteria.

Labeling is not a substitute for regulatory compliance. Labels wouldn't be awarded to products, for example, that were unsafe or did not meet regulatory requirements. To qualify for a labeling program, a product must first comply with the relevant environmental regulations in the country where it was manufactured and with the relevant product-related environmental regulations of the country where it is marketed.

Definitions in ISO/CD 14024

A few key definitions in the standard include the following. Again, note that since the standard is in the development stage, the following definitions could change.

Product criteria.   A "set of qualitative and quantitative technical requirements that the applicant, product or product category shall meet to be awarded an environmental label. Product criteria include ecological and product function elements."

Product.   Goods and services for consumer, commercial, and industrial purposes.

Product function.   Attributes and characteristics in the use of a product.

Product category.   Groups of products which serve similar purposes or have equivalent use from the consumer's point of view.

Selecting Product Categories

The first step in a typical labeling program is to select which product categories should be eligible for the labels. The standard describes the considerations involved in this process. A few of the major ones include the following.

A key issue is whether awarding a label will actually reduce the environmental impacts of the products in the category. That is, if a label is awarded to a product in a category, are there similar products that have the potential for environmental improvement? Some labeling programs exclude a whole class of products, such as household chemicals, because of the negative environmental impact of all products in the class.

Another issue is market volume and market share. An obvious implication is that there must be significant market volume in the category of products applying for the label for the award to have appeal and credibility.

Procedures for Setting Criteria

Another major step in labeling programs is to develop criteria for each product category. The aim of labeling procedures is uniformity in developing criteria, based on proven technical and scientific assessment, for different product categories.

Selectivity. According to the draft standard, an effective program is selective. That is, it must set criteria high enough so that, although some products can meet the criteria, many others cannot. This stimulates competition and increases public confidence in the program. The ISO/CD 14024 draft standard states that multiple-criteria labeling programs should select criteria that distinguish leading products from alternatives for every product category.

Decisions about market share come into play when setting threshold criteria. If the criteria are set too high, the award of the label is restricted to products with a small market share. If the criteria are set too low, the label will be awarded to a much larger percentage of the market.

Flexibility. According to the standard, the criteria for awarding the label shouldn't be locked in stone but should be periodically reviewed to take into account new technologies, new products, or other factors. Also, the criteria are reviewed to set the threshold level higher, to increase competition, and to stimulate product improvement.

Consultation/accessibility. Labeling programs should establish some formal and public method for consulting with their stakeholders when selecting criteria and defining product categories. All interested parties should be able to apply to and participate in environmental labeling programs. At the same time, although labeling programs should be transparent, they must also protect confidential business information. Information gathered from applicant companies should not be disclosed without written permission of the applicant.

Final Consultation, Adoption, and Publication

When the practitioner has set the product categories and criteria, it should publish the proposed criteria, accompanied by a document that indicates that the criteria are objective and verifiable, their development conforms with the scope, principles, and framework of the ISO 14024 standard, and that interested parties, including foreign and domestic producers, were invited to be part of the process and their views were taken into consideration.

Guidelines for Certification Procedures

The standard lays out some guidelines for the actual certification procedures that involve assessing the conformity of the submitted products against the criteria. A primary consideration is that the testing organization or similar body that performs the conformity assessment must be able to verify all elements of the program's criteria. The program should use either ISO standards or "repeatable and reproducible" methods that follow accepted principles of good laboratory practice.

Awarding the Label

If the applicant complies with the general rules of the program and the product complies with the specific product criteria, the practitioner issues the applicant a license to use the label on specified products.

The standard notes that issuing a license does not obligate the licensee to use the label. In some cases, the licensee may be satisfied if a product fulfills the criteria. It is up to the practitioners to maintain a publicly available list of licensed products.

ISO/CD 14021—ENVIRONMENTAL LABELING— SELF-DECLARATION ENVIRONMENTAL CLAIMS—TERMS AND DEFINITIONS

WG2 is working on self-declaration environmental claims. The first proposed standard, ISO/CD 14021, focuses on terms and definitions. The standard has two goals:

- To establish general guidelines regarding environmental claims in relation to the supply of goods and services.
- To define and provide rules for the use of specific terms used in environmental claims.

The scope of the standard does not preclude or override legally required environmental information, claims, or labeling. For example, many countries have specific legal requirements that apply to packaging. The United States has rules about misleading advertising and making false claims. The Federal Trade Commission (FTC) has also issued guidelines for environmental claims that are generally consistent with those in this standard.[1]

What Is a Self-Declaration Environmental Claim?

An environmental claim is defined in the ISO/CD 14021 standard as any "environmental declaration that describes or implies by whatever means the effects that the raw material extraction, production, distribution, use, or disposal of a product or service has on the environment." The definition applies to local, regional, and global effects. The environment is that which an individual lives in, affects, or is affected by.

A self-declaration environmental claim is "an environmental claim that is made, without independent third-party certification, by manufacturers, importers, distributors, retailers, or anyone else likely to benefit from such a claim." Claims can take the form of statements, symbols, or graphics on product or package labels, product literature, technical bulletins, advertising, television, and so on.

Definitions in ISO/CD 14021

Explanatory statement.   Any further explanation which is needed so that an environmental claim can be properly understood by a purchaser or consumer.

Package/packaging.   A material or item that is used to protect or contain, a product during transportation, storage, or marketing. A package can also be a material item that is physically attached to, or included with, a product or its container for the purpose of marketing the product or communicating information about the product.

Qualified environmental claim.   A qualified claim or environmental claim is one that "is accompanied by an explanatory statement that describes the limits of the claim."

Objectives and Benefits

The primary objective of the standard is to contribute to the reduction of environmental burdens and impacts associated with the consumption of goods and services. The specific objective is to harmonize the use of environmental claims. The standard lists some anticipated benefits:

- Accurate, verifiable, nondeceptive environmental claims.
- Increased potential for market forces to stimulate environmental improvements in product, process, and service delivery.
- More informed choices by purchasers and consumers.
- Prevention or minimization of unwarranted claims.
- Reduction in marketplace confusion.
- Reduction in trade restrictions and barriers.

General Guidelines and Criteria for Self-Declaration Claims

The draft standard lists several guidelines for the use of self-declaration claims and any explanatory statements. A few of the major ones include the following:

Accurate, nondeceptive, substantiated, and verifiable. The claim should be accurate and nondeceptive. It should be substantiated, that is, supported by appropriate evidence and verifiable. Verification methods should be reproducible, repeatable, and scientifically sound. Testing and verification methods will be addressed in the ISO 14023 standard when it is developed by Working Group 2.

Relevant. The claim should be relevant to the particular product or service and used only in an appropriate context or setting. It should relate to an actual, not potential, environmental benefit. Environmental claims must be relevant to the geographic area where the corresponding environmental effect will occur. For example, a claim about the manufacture of a product should be relevant to the area where the product was made. A claim made in relation to the benefits flowing from the use, recycling, or disposal of the product should be relevant to the area where it is sold.

Specific and clear. The claim should be specific and clear as to what particular environmental improvement and attribute it relates to. It should be unlikely to be misinterpreted. Claims that are literally true but are likely to be misinterpreted by purchasers should not be used. In particular, these include claims that can be misleading through omission of relevant facts.

Claims must not suggest an environmental improvement that does not exist or exaggerate the environmental benefit of an attribute of the products and services to which the claim refers, especially if it's negligible. An example of the first situation would be a paper bag that is labeled recyclable. Such paper bags are usually not separated in landfills and thus are not likely to actually be recycled. The claim refers to an environmental benefit that is negligible or nonexistent.

An example of exaggeration would be a manufacturer who says that a package has "100 percent more recycled content." Actually, the recycled content of the package has been increased from 2 percent to 4 percent. Though the claim is technically true, it is misleading and gives an exaggerated impression.

Claims should not be made on the presence or absence of ingredients or features which have never been associated with that product category.

If an environmental claim applies only to the product, or only to the packaging, the components of the product or packaging, or in relation to the provision of a service, this must be made clear. That is, if only the packaging and not the product is recyclable, the claim must clearly indicate this. An example would be a box of aluminum foil that simply said it was recyclable without indicating whether the claim refers to the box or the foil.

Comparative assertions. Any environmental claim that involves a comparative assertion of environmental superiority or improvement must be specific, valid, and make clear the basis for the comparison. In particular, it should be relevant to how recently any improvement was made. The comparison should only be made with a published standard or products or services of the same kind supplied by the same or another producer.

A specific comparative statement would be "our package contains 40 percent more recycled content than our previous package" rather than merely the statement "40 percent more recycled content." A claim that says "the least waste of all leading brands" must be substantiated by objective information.

General environmental claims. The ISO/CD 14021 standard warns against the use of general and vague terms that have little or no real meaning, such as "environmentally safe," "environmentally friendly," "earth friendly," "green," and so on. These are misleading in that almost no product is actually good for the environment. The issue is which products are relatively less harmful. Also, vague terms cannot be substantiated or verified. They lead consumers to make unwarranted assumptions.

Specific Terms

The major section of the ISO/CD 14021 standard defines specific terms commonly used in environmental claims. Each definition is accompanied by qualifications or limitations concerning its use. Since the standard is still in development, the definitions may change and are not described in this chapter.

SYMBOLS, AND TESTING AND VERIFICATION METHODS

As mentioned earlier, Working Group 2 has two other projects on its plate: a standard on the use of symbols in claims and one on testing and verification methods. Discussions have begun on the symbols document and work is anticipated shortly on testing and verification methods. Further revision of the ISO/CD 14021 standard will not take place until the work on symbols and on testing and verification methods proceeds.

ISSUES TO RESOLVE

There are many issues raised by the labeling efforts of Subcommittee 3. Here are a few of the primary ones under discussion by the standards developers.

Information or Improvement?

A key issue goes to the heart of the effort—what is the primary purpose of environmental labeling? Is it to convey accurate information to consumers so that they can make informed decisions? Or is it to improve the environmental performance of industrial operations? Actually, most people would agree that both of these are worthy goals. The issue is how environmental performance is achieved and what role labeling plays in that process.

Debate during the drafting process has focused on how explicitly these goals should be included in the standards themselves and the weight accorded to each goal.[2] The issue was resolved in some measure in the ISO/CD 14020 draft standard. What was in earlier drafts a separate principle is now a statement in the Introduction: "The overall goal of the 14000 series is to lessen the stress placed on the environment by the production, use and disposal of products and services using a system of continual environmental improvement." The underlying debate, however, is likely to remain. The argument for an explicit acknowledgment of environmental improvement is based on the notion that without such a statement, the standards would have no point. The entire labeling effort is a market-based attempt to improve the environmental performance of industry.

On the other side are those who favor the communication goal—that the primary purpose of labeling is to provide accurate and effective communication of the environmental aspects of products to consumers. Consumers, in turn, can use this information to weigh environmental considerations against other legitimate factors, such as cost, durability, safety, emotional appeal, or even competing environmental considerations.

Environmental improvement may or may not be a possible goal, and the actual reduction of environmental burdens as a result of labeling may or may not be an outcome. But these are not the only goals of labeling, according to this view. For example, if the explicit goal was environmental improvement, a manufacturer couldn't make a purely descriptive claim about a product.

This last point reflects an industry concern. Manufacturers often have objectives other than environmental improvement that prompt them to make claims. Some industries believe that labeling programs create pressures on manufacturers to go beyond regulatory requirements that apply to their products, without any demonstrable environmental improvements as a result. One reason is that the methods and practices of labeling programs are not rigorous or scientific enough to provide confidence that products receiving the label actually are less harmful to the environment. Thus, the emphasis in the labeling standards, from industry's point of view, should be on increasing the technical rigor of labeling program procedures.

Consistency with Regulations

A common concern is that the international standards should be consistent with domestic requirements and guidelines. An example in the United States is the FTC's guidelines for marketing terms, referred to earlier in this chapter. Consistency between international standards and national laws is important to widespread acceptance and adoption of the standards.

Trade Barriers and GATT

The goal of avoiding trade barriers that result from labeling programs was one of the principles mentioned in ISO/CD 14020. Most labeling programs use some kind of life cycle assessment to establish the labeling criteria. These assessments relate to process and production methods (for example, textiles produced with nonpolluting dyes or furniture made from wood harvested from forests that were managed according to sustainable techniques).

If the criteria specifies certain process and production methods (PPMs) and foreign producers can't comply with the criteria due to their different production methods, the labeling program may give rise to trade barriers. This is especially problematic for developing countries whose manufacturers may not be able to comply with such requirements. For one thing, the criteria and thresholds may be so restrictive that a sophisticated technology is required which developing countries either do not have or cannot afford. It may also entail use of alternative raw materials that may lead to increased costs.[3]

The General Agreement on Tariffs and Trade (GATT) includes, in its section on Technical Barriers to Trade, rules concerning trade barriers resulting from the use of standards. The rules, however, are not completely clear in their application to the issue of PPMs.

Trade issues in general are of growing interest and concern, not only in TC 207 but worldwide. SC3 is examining the trade barrier issues in more detail.

Where Does Labeling Fit into the ISO 14000 System?

When a company is registered to ISO 14001 and receives a certificate, the marketplace has some confidence that the company has in place a management process to control its environmental issues. Furthermore, an accreditation body has judged that the registrar (certifier) awarding the registration is competent to do its job.

A labeling claim, however, goes to the environmental attributes of a product and the claim appears on the product and/or the packaging. How does the consumer know that the labeling program that awarded the label is competent and, therefore, that the label is valid and credible? Will the labeling program advertise that its methods conform to the ISO 14024 standard? Should labeling programs seek third-party certification for conformance to buttress this claim? If so, will there be third-party certification to the labeling standards for practitioner programs? What about third-party certification for self-declaration claims?

CONCLUSION

It's too early to predict the answers to the above questions or even the extent to which the ISO standards will be accepted worldwide. Interest in environmental labeling, however, appears to be growing and environmental claims of all types are likely to play a larger role in marketing products. The labeling standards, when fully developed and adopted, have the potential to add credibility to labeling programs and increase consumer confidence in the results.

NOTES

1. U.S. Federal Trade Commission. *Guides for the Use of Environmental Marketing Claims,* July 1992.

2. In addition to observing the debates on this issue, many of the points raised in this section are based on discussions and comments by US delegates to TC 207 including Chris Bell, Joe Cascio, Arthur Weissman, and Jim Connaughton.

3. Ralph Luken, Octavio Maizza-Neto, and Lars Aumann, "Environmental Management Systems and Eco-Labeling: Potential Adverse Effects on the Trade of Developing Countries," paper presented at ISO/CASCO Conformity Assessment for Environmental Management Workshop, June 12–13, 1995, Geneva, Switzerland.

Chapter Ten

Environmental Aspects in Product Standards

Unlike the ISO 14000 series, the vast majority of standards that ISO develops are product technical standards (i.e., how long should the prongs on a electric plug be, what are the specifications for a tool, etc.). Product standards often affect every detail of a product. Thousands of standards developers work on drafting such standards every year.

Product standards have environmental implications and increasingly, environmental issues are playing a role in product design and product development. Design for the Environment (DfE) is becoming a useful tool for companies to improve their products, the efficiency of their production methods, and the environmental aspects of their products.

The implication is that product standards writers ought to be aware of the environmental implications of their work. TC 207 formed a separate working group, WG1 Environmental Aspects in Product Standards, to look at this issue.

WG1 is developing a guideline document, *ISO/CD 14060 Guide for the inclusion of environmental aspects in product standards,* for use by standards writers on the environmental aspects of product standards. The guideline document is neither a technical standard that prescribes requirements that products must meet, nor is it a management standard in the ISO 14001 mode that includes management specifications.

PURPOSE AND SCOPE

The purpose of the guideline is to describe some general considerations that product standards developers should take into account. These considerations balance two goals: achieving the intended product performance and reducing adverse environmental effects that may arise. The objectives of the WG1, as outlined in the guideline, are to:

- Raise awareness that provisions in product standards can affect the environment, both negatively and positively.
- Outline the relationship between product standards and the environment.
- Help avoid provisions in product standards that may adversely affect the environment.
- Emphasize that addressing environmental aspects in product standards is a complex process and requires balancing competing priorities.
- Recommend the use of life cycle thinking and recognized scientific methodologies in developing product standards that incorporate environmental aspects.

The guideline outlines ways in which provisions in product standards may affect the environment during the stages of a product's life cycle. It does not require that developers use LCA, but describes the concept and the general process.

The standard also addresses some methods that standards writers can use to identify and assess the environmental effects of provisions in product standards.

Finally, it highlights some strategies for improving environmental performance. It focuses on raising awareness of three environmental improvement strategies: resource conservation, pollution prevention, and design for the environment.

AUDIENCE

The intended audience for the standard is product standards writers. These include a broad range of professionals, including engineers, technicians, members of industry associations, industry representatives, and others. The standard is not designed to educate the audience in every aspect of the subject or to be overly prescriptive. The aim is to raise awareness. Product standards writers will probably need expert assistance to actually apply the guidelines.

STATUS

The *ISO/CD 14060 Guide for the inclusion of environmental aspects in product standards* has been submitted for approval as an ISO guide. As discussed in Chapter 11 on conformity assessment, ISO guides are not standards; they are guidelines published by ISO's Committee on Conformity Assessment (CASCO). The International Electrotechnical Commission (IEC), which is ISO's counterpart in the electronics area, is also developing a guide similar to this, *Guide 02.594 Environmental aspects— inclusion in electrotechnical product standards.* The IEC guide is meant to complement the more general ISO/CD 14060 standard and is tailored to the special needs of electrical/electronics products.

SYNOPSIS OF THE GUIDELINE

The introduction to the guideline points out that every product has some effect on the environment during its manufacture, distribution, use, or disposal. Provisions in product standards can influence significantly the extent of these environmental effects. By product, the standard refers to "products, processes, services, and combinations thereof."

The standard cautions that anticipating and identifying a product's environmental effects is a complex process, and there's little agreement on environmental cause and effect relationships. A product's environmental effects are interrelated, and emphasizing a single effect can alter environmental effects at other stages of the product's life cycle.

General Considerations

Given these caveats, however, standards writers should consider a product's environmental effects when developing standards. Provisions in the standards should reflect strategies such as pollution prevention and resource conservation, intended uses, and reasonably foreseeable misuses.

These effects should be balanced against other factors, including the product's function, performance, safety and health impact, cost, marketability, and quality.

The guideline points out that product innovation rates are high. Therefore, product standards should be reviewed whenever new knowledge can benefit the environment. At the same time, standards writers should avoid provisions that are too prescriptive; this can stifle innovation and environmental improvements. For example, the standard warns against specifying materials to be used in product standards. This can preclude innovation and hinder manufacturers from selecting alternate materials that are better for the environment. Provisions in standards also shouldn't preclude the appropriate use of secondary or recycled materials.

How Provisions in Product Standards Can Influence the Environment

Products can affect the environment at different stages of their life cycle. Provisions in product standards to some extent determine relevant environmental aspects peculiar to the product. They can both facilitate and hamper environmental improvement.

The requirements in product standards, either descriptive or performance, affect the choices made during the design and production of a new or improved product. The guideline lists several choices that standards can influence:

- Material and energy inputs.
- Type and quantity of waste and releases generated.
- Inputs and outputs associated with packaging, transportation, distribution, and use.
- Options for recovery, such as reuse, recycling, ease of disassembly, repair, and restoration.
- Options for disposal of the product.

The guideline points out that provisions should be no more or less stringent than necessary to achieve the product's purpose to avoid excessive or inefficient material or energy use.

Environmental Effects to Consider in Product Standards Development

The standard discusses the environmental effects generated during the product's life cycle. These effects are determined by the inputs used and the outputs generated at all stages of the product's life cycle.

There are two categories of inputs: materials and energy. Both types are used throughout most of the life cycle. Material inputs can produce a variety of effects, such as depletion of renewable and nonrenewable resources, impaired land use, excessive waste and emissions to air, effluents to water, and other releases.

Energy inputs refer to fossil fuels, nuclear, hydroelectric, geothermal, thermal waste recovery, and other types, each of which has environmental effects. Outputs other than the product itself include air emissions, water effluents, solid waste, and other releases.

Significant environmental effects include depletion of renewable and nonrenewable resources, impaired land use, environmental or human exposure to hazardous materials, excessive waste and emissions to air, effluents to water, and other harmful releases.

How to Identify and Assess Environmental Effects

The guideline recommends the use of life cycle assessment thinking, with the caveat that a complete understanding of LCA methods and their limitations requires extensive experience. It also warns that the "relevance and value of the methodology . . . will vary depending upon the product and the product sector involved." If the LCA analysis is applied improperly or in abbreviated form, an incomplete or distorted picture of the environmental effects and trade-offs associated with a product may result.

The guideline recommends a general familiarity with LCA methods to provide a basic understanding of how product standards provisions may influence a product's environmental effects.

Product Standards and Environmental Improvement Strategies

The guideline looks at three major strategies for environmental improvement: resource conservation, prevention of pollution, and design for environment.

Resource Conservation

Resource conservation generally means reducing the depletion of both renewable and nonrenewable resources. The less that is depleted, the better. Renewable resources such as timber can be replaced much faster than a nonrenewable resource such as fossil fuel. Considerations in conserving resources involve:

- The environmental effects of energy sources.
- The conversion efficiency of a selected source.

Once an energy source is selected, another consideration is to maximize efficiency. Each energy source has an inherent energy content and the goal in resource conservation is to minimize the loss of inherent energy.

Prevention of Pollution

The guideline emphasizes that human and industrial activity results in releases to air, land, and/or water and lists the various ways to reduce these releases. It also points out that there are developing environmental problems about which there is no international consensus, such as climate change, ozone depletion, and some ecological effects. The guideline cautions standards writers to "consider sector-specific expertise when addressing these issues until further consensus has been reached on an international level."

Design for the Environment

The guideline encourages standards writers to be aware of evolving techniques such as design for the environment (DfE). For example, DfE incorporates approaches that are part of product concept, need, and design. Considerations used in DfE involve material substitution, reuse, maintainability, and design for disassembly and recyclability.

CONCLUSION

This brief description of the environmental aspects in product standards guideline brings our discussion of the product and process evaluation standards to a close. The next part of this book looks at implementing ISO 14000 and the registration process.

IV

ENVIRONMENTAL MANAGEMENT
Implementation

Internal Organization for Standardization
Technical Committee 207

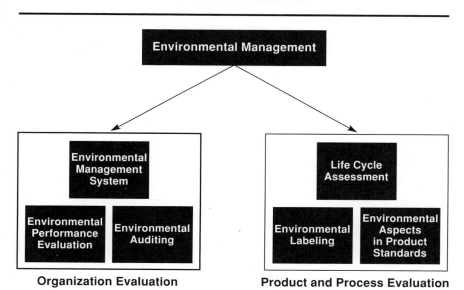

Organization Evaluation   Product and Process Evaluation

Chapter Eleven

ISO 14000 Registration and Conformity Assessment

Although suitable for self-declaration and second-party use, the ISO 14001 specification standard has been drafted in anticipation of its use in third-party registration (certification). This chapter looks briefly at the registration process and at related conformity assessment issues, including:

- Who ensures the competency of ISO 14000 registrars? That is, who accredits registrars?
- What criteria are used in the accreditation process?
- Who ensures the competence of ISO 14000 auditors and the consistent interpretation of ISO 14000 standards?
- Under what conditions are ISO 14001 certificates recognized and accepted worldwide?

It's important to note that ISO confines its work to the development of international standards. It has no direct responsibility for setting up the framework for assessing the conformity of EMS programs to ISO 14000 requirements. The infrastructure of conformity assessment comprises national testing and certification bodies, and accreditation bodies set up specifically to ensure the credibility and effectiveness of third-party registration.

THE PROBABLE REGISTRATION PROCESS

What Is Third-Party Registration?

Third-party registration is the assessment of an EMS by independent auditors associated with an organization qualified to perform EMS audits. This organization is referred to as a registrar or registration (certification) body.

Different categories of registrars are likely to offer ISO 14000 registration services. One category is likely to be registrars who now offer ISO 9000 quality systems registration. Others could include large accounting firms, consulting companies, or organizations set up specifically to provide ISO 14000 registration services.[1]

What Is Registered?

Does registration cover the facility, site, or entire corporation? Recall that EMAS focused at the site level. ISO 14001 is more flexible. Essentially, it is up to the organization to define the scope of its EMS. The scope of registration can be site-specific, apply to operations that are part of a site, to divisions at several sites, or to the entire company.

Steps in the Registration Process

The registration process for ISO 14001 has not been fully developed yet. Based on the ISO 9000 process, however, and current EMS registration to the UK's BS 7750 standard, the registration process for ISO 14001 is likely to include the following steps.[2]

Application. An application to the registrar usually begins the process. Sometimes a contract is signed. Before the application is approved, the organization and the registrar work out some key issues, such as the scope of the proposed registration, the time frame, the size of the company, and other basic issues.

Registrars are accredited by their accreditation organizations to register companies in certain industrial classifications. The organization applying to a registrar must make certain the registrar is accredited and competent to perform audits in their industry sector. The registrar's scope is determined by reference to some classification system. In the United States, for instance, the Standard Industrial Classification (SIC) Codes are used. In Europe, a similar system of codes, Nomenclature Generale des Activites Economiques Dan les Communautes Europeenes (NACE), is used to define scope.

Initial review of documents. Another typical element is an initial review of the organization's existing documents, such as their environmental management manual and other documents that demonstrate the presence of an EMS program that conforms to ISO 14001 requirements. This "paper audit" usually takes place at the registrar's offices, not on site.

Preassessment. Many registrars conduct preassessments. Some registrars require them. Usually, the purpose of a preassessment is to determine whether a company's EMS is ready for the complete audit. Also, it helps the registrar plan for the full audit, in terms of the size and makeup of the audit team and the length of time required for the audit.

Registrars are prohibited from consulting with the client company during a preassessment. The registrar may evaluate the state of the organization's EMS and check it against ISO 14001 requirements. But the registrar can't provide guidance. It can, however, uncover obvious areas where the organization is deficient and thus, not ready yet for the full audit. This gives the organization an opportunity to correct the deficiencies.

Assessment. The next element is the full audit. This can take several days and involve a group of auditors. If the client wants both an ISO 9000 and ISO 14000 certificate, the majority of registrars will probably conduct a single, extended audit to cover both the quality and the environmental management systems. This could take several additional days.

Registration. In most registration processes, there are three possible outcomes.

Approval. The company's EMS will be registered to ISO 14001 if it has implemented all the elements of the standard and has only what the registrar considers minor deficiencies—those that the existing EMS is well equipped to correct.

Conditional or provisional approval. A company will probably be either conditionally or provisionally approved if:

- It has addressed all the elements of the standard and has documented its systems, but perhaps not fully implemented them.
- A number of deficiencies detected in a particular area show a negative, systemic trend.

Conditional approval requires the company to respond to any deficiencies noted during the time frame defined by the registrar. The registrar, upon evaluating the company's corrective action, may elect to perform an on-site reevaluation or accept the corrective action in writing and review the implementation in conjunction with subsequent surveillance visits.

Disapproval. The final possibility is disapproval, which usually occurs when a company's system is either very well documented but has not been implemented, or when entire elements of the standard have not been addressed at all. This situation will definitely require a comprehensive reevaluation by the registrar prior to issuing registration.

Once a company is registered, the company receives a certificate and is listed in a register or directory published by the registrar or another organization. The company should also expect to receive rules for use of the certificate at this time.

Surveillance Audits

It is important for a company pursuing registration to understand the duration and/or validity of its registration. Some registrars offer registrations that are valid indefinitely, pending continuing successful surveillance visits. Others offer registrations valid for a specific time, such as three or four years.

Most registrars conduct surveillance every six months. Those whose registrations expire conduct either a complete reassessment at the end of the registration period, or an assessment that is somewhere between a surveillance visit and a complete reaudit. The client should clearly understand the registrar's policy in this area.

During the interval between surveillance visits, the company should continually ensure that its demonstrated EMS is in place and operating, so that the surveillance visit will merely confirm the fact. Of course, the EMS audit and the management review requirements in ISO 14001 would assist the organization to maintain and improve its system.

Combined Audits for ISO 9000 and ISO 14000

Organizations that have existing ISO 9000–registered sites or who plan to implement both sets of standards are understandably interested in a single, comprehensive audit for both standards. As one expert put it, "companies want one audit, one audit team, one report covering ISO 9001 and ISO 14001 management systems, two certificates, and one bill!"[3]

How Long Does ISO 14001 Implementation Take?

This varies widely with the type and size of the organization and how developed its existing EMS system is. Again, based on experience in the ISO 9000 arena, implementation can take anywhere from 6 to 24 months, with 12 months as a general average.

How Long Is the Registration Period?

The registration certificate is usually valid for three years, although this can vary. Some registrars issue indefinite certificates, pending continuing successful surveillance visits. In most cases, registrars conduct surveillance audits on a six-month schedule. When a certificate expires, the certification body conducts either another complete reassessment or an assessment that is between a surveillance visit and a complete reassessment.

How Much Does Registration Cost?

Registration costs fall into two categories: internal implementation costs and external costs such as the hiring of consultants and the cost of the actual registration audit. Any projection of costs at this point would be strictly speculative. Using ISO 9000 experience again as a very rough guideline, the cost of a registration audit falls within the range of $10,000–$30,000, depending on the size of the facility and the nature of its operations. Internal implementation costs vary widely with the particular company. In an ISO 9000 survey conducted by Deloitte Touche and Quality Systems Update ISO 9000 Information Service, internal implementation costs among respondents ranged from less than $100,000 to over $600,000. The average cost reported was $245,200.[4]

Use of the Certificate

The ISO 14001 registration certificate can be used in marketing and advertising. It is not a product certification nor an environmental label and therefore cannot be displayed on a product or its packaging. ISO has published rules regarding the proper use of registration certificates in the quality field.

REGISTRAR ACCREDITATION

The credibility of the ISO 14000 process will depend to a large measure on the competence of the ISO 14000 registrar (certifying body). Who ensures the competence of registrars, and using what criteria? This is usually determined by accreditation.

Figure 11–1 illustrates the registration-accreditation-recognition hierarchy. The companies are at the bottom. Their EMS systems are audited by the registrars, at the next level. The registrars' competence is assured by accreditors. At the top of the hierarchy are the governmental authorities or quasi-governmental authorities that recognize the competence of the accreditors.

What Is Accreditation?

Accreditation is the initial evaluation and periodic monitoring of a registrar's competence, performed by an accreditation body. Accreditation bodies are either in operation in most countries or in development. A few well-known

FIGURE 11–1
The Registration/Accreditation/Recognition Hierarchy

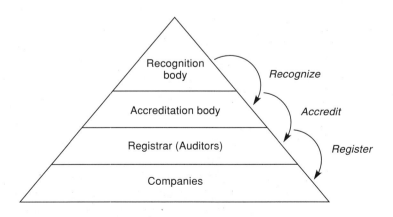

accreditors include the United Kingdom Accreditation Service (UKAS) (formerly known as the National Accreditation Council for Certification Bodies [NACCB]), the Dutch Council for Certification (RvC) in The Netherlands, and the Registrar Accreditation Board (RAB) in the United States.

Accreditation of ISO 14000 Registrars (Certifiers)

In the United Kingdom, the official accreditation body for BS 7750 EMS registration (certification) is UKAS. In the United States, an accreditation body has not yet been formed. Organizations that have expressed an interest include the Registrar Accreditation Board (RAB), the Environmental Auditing Roundtable (EAR), and the American National Standards Institute (ANSI) itself. It is possible that more than one organization could divide the responsibilities. For example, RAB could handle registrar accreditation while the EAR would be tasked with auditor certification.

Accreditation Criteria

Accreditation bodies use established criteria against which to evaluate the competence of registrars (certifiers). For example, quality system registrars are evaluated against the requirements of the EN 45000 series of standards, developed by CEN/CENELEC.

Particularly relevant is *EN 45012, General criteria for certification bodies operating quality system certification,* which sets out key criteria for registrars. Most accreditation bodies use EN 45012 to evaluate the competence of registrars. This standard is being adapted for use in the ISO 14000 context.

Other guidance for accreditation of registrars and for the assessment of accreditors themselves is contained in CASCO guides. CASCO is ISO's Committee on Conformity Assessment. It has developed several guides that are adopted by organizations for use in accreditation and certification. One such guide is *ISO/IEC Guide 48, Guidelines for a third-party assessment and registration of a supplier's quality system.* (Other relevant guides are described in the adjoining Box.)

CASCO and CASCO Guides

CASCO is the conformity assessment committee of ISO. Its goals are to:

- Study means of assessing the conformity of products, processes, services, and quality systems to appropriate standards or other technical specifications.

- Prepare international guides relating to the testing, inspection, and certification of products, processes, and services, and to the assessment of quality systems, testing laboratories, inspection bodies, certification bodies, and their operation and acceptance.

- Promote mutual recognition and acceptance of national and regional conformity assessment systems and the appropriate use of international standards for testing, inspection, certification, assessment, and related purposes.

CASCO guides are developed by working groups of experts from around the world using a consensus process. These guides serve as a basis for national practices. They are used by suppliers, conformity assessment bodies, accreditors, approval bodies and trade policy makers.

CASCO guide usage should increase since all members of the new World Trade Organization must adhere to the chapter on Technical Barriers to Trade. That chapter of the GATT agreement specifically cites the use of international guides for conformity assessment.

Three CASCO guides under development or revision that are relevant to environmental management system registration include:

ISO/CASCO 226 (rev 2). General requirements for assessment and accreditation of certification/registration bodies.

ISO/CASCO 227 (rev 2). General requirements for bodies operating assessment and certification/registration of quality systems.

ISO/CASCO 228 (rev 2). General requirements for bodies operating product certification systems.

Recognition of the Accreditation Body

At the top of the hierarchy is government or other quasi-government recognition of the accreditation body itself. In the United States, the National Institute of Standards and Technology (NIST) has recognized RAB as the official accreditation body for ISO 9000 registrars. In the future, NIST may also recognize the ISO 14001 registrar accreditation body.

RECOGNITION OF THE ISO 14001 CERTIFICATE

An accredited and competent registrar should conduct a professional audit and issue a credible ISO 14001 registration certificate. The next question that could arise is this: Will the certificate be recognized and accepted worldwide in those areas where the company does business?

There's no guarantee that all ISO 14001 certificates will be viewed as equally valuable. For example, will an ISO 14001 certificate earned by a company in a country with extensive and rigorously enforced environmental laws be viewed as valuable as a certificate from a country with a weak regulatory system or a strong system that is not enforced?

It's too early to tell how ISO 14001 certificates will be accepted; however, if ISO 9000 is a useful precedent, the basic guidelines may be as follows.

If an organization's customers recognize its ISO 14001 certificate, no matter which registrar awarded it, that may be sufficient. The marketplace ultimately determines the acceptability of a certificate.

The reputation of the registrar may be a factor in the acceptability of a certificate. Companies can "shop" for the services of the registrar they perceive to be the most qualified and most credible.

The credibility of a registrar is affected by its accreditation status. There is no automatic acceptance of ISO 9000 certificates among registrars or among accreditation bodies. Acceptance of the certificates depends on mutual recognition agreements. Many registrars and accreditation bodies around the world, however, are developing such agreements.

There is also a proposal for an international system of recognition, the Quality System Assessment Recognition, that would lead to worldwide recognition of ISO 9000 registration certificate. This system, now under development, is based on the goal of having a single ISO 9000 registration certificate that is recognized and accepted anywhere in the world, regardless of the location of either client or registration body.

AUDITOR COMPETENCE

A final key issue is the competence and professionalism of the ISO 14000 auditors. Who will certify their competence? And according to what standards? How can customers be confident that auditors are consistently interpreting and applying the ISO 14000 standards? How will auditors deal with the wide variability in EMS programs in developed and developing countries? Auditors will be expected to audit the EMS but not the environmental performance of the company. If they find problems, what will their responsibility be?

Consistent interpretation of the standard will be a big challenge. There are many concepts in the standards that are open to interpretation, such as environmental aspects and continual improvement.

In the ISO 9000 context, the ISO 10011 auditing standards, *Guidelines for auditing quality systems,* have been accepted by most registrars and accreditation bodies. ISO 10011 has three parts: *Part 1: Auditing; Part 2: Qualification criteria for quality system auditors; and Part 3: Management of audit programs.* Similarly, the ISO 14010–12 auditing standards are likely to be adopted worldwide to assist in the performance of consistent and competent audits.

In addition, auditors are being certified in many programs worldwide. Two of these in the quality area include the Institute for Quality Assurance's (IQA) National Registration Scheme for Assessors of Quality Systems in the United Kingdom and the RAB's Certification Program for Auditors of Quality Systems in the United States. In addition, the International Auditor Training and Certification Association (IATCA) was formed in 1993 to develop an international set of requirements for quality management system audits.

Challenges for EMS Auditors

UKAS in the United Kingdom (formerly known as the NACCB) began to accredit BS 7750 registration/certification bodies in March 1995 by accrediting the first eight registrars. In January, 1995, UKAS published The Environmental Accreditation Criteria. These are based on the requirements of EN 45012. As part of the development process, NACCB assessed more than 40 certification bodies. This experience may shed some light on the challenges faced by registration auditors.[5]

Process, not performance. A familiar issue by now is the degree to which auditors assess the management process rather than the environmental performance output. UKAS's criteria do not recommend that the assessment or judgment of performance be the basis for certification.[6]

Yet, commentators imply that process can't be easily separated from performance and that effective ISO 14001 auditors, in addition to basic understanding of management elements, will need a technical understanding of environmental performance issues, specialized environmental knowledge and experience, and the ability to evaluate environmental aspects and impacts.

Auditors will need to understand issues such as the nature of the organization's regulatory compliance, its performance measuring systems, its significant environmental impacts, and other aspects of environmental performance.

The implication is that ISO 14000 auditors, more so than ISO 9000 auditors, may not go as far as to judge environmental performance but may have to go beyond ensuring that basic management elements, such as policies, manuals, and procedures, are in place.[7]

Key areas. The UKAS criteria point out some key areas of the EMS that both the organization and auditors should focus on. These include:

- Has the organization identified and evaluated environmental aspects in a systematic way?
- Have objectives and targets been set in such a way that they can be compared to actual performance?
- Is environmental performance being monitored and reported appropriate to the objectives and targets?
- Are audits focusing on the environmental management system?
- Is there evidence of corrective action and management system improvement resulting from audit information?

Assessing regulatory compliance. If a site is not in compliance with regulations, will it achieve certification? Since few sites are completely in compliance, the question that experts have posed is: What level of noncompliance do auditors accept? A major violation? Several small violations? One opinion is that as long as a site has an EMS in place that allows it to comply within a reasonable time frame and correct violations, it should meet the standard.[8]

Also, if the auditor discovers a violation, is he or she responsible for reporting it to management? If not, what is the auditor's legal liability, if any? If yes, what type of violation should be reported? Questions concerning the nature and extent of an auditor's legal responsibilities will take experience to fully resolve.

Generally, experts agree that violations should be reported to management but not to anyone else. This is called for in the ISO 14010–14011 standards. Once the auditor reports the violation, it becomes management's responsibility to report the violations to the appropriate regulatory agency.

CONCLUSION

Even the brief discussion in this chapter is evidence enough that conformity assessment issues are complex. The success of the ISO 14000 movement and confidence in the usefulness of the ISO 14000 certificate will depend on consistent and credible conformity assessment procedures. Registrars using the BS 7750 standard now and those who will use the ISO 14000 standards shortly are gathering experience that will help resolve the conformity assessment issues. In addition, CASCO and many other groups are hard at work to create the mechanisms that will support the successful implementation of ISO 14000 worldwide.

NOTES

1. The Quality Systems Update ISO 9000 Information Service conducted a survey of US-based registrars in July 1995. Of the 30 respondents to the survey, all 30 planned to seek accreditation to offer ISO 14001 registration services. *Quality Systems Update ISO 14000 Environmental Management Standards Registrar Survey,* July 1995.

2. Adapted from Elizabeth Potts, "Steps in the Registration Process," *ISO 9000 Handbook, 2nd ed.,* ed. Robert W. Peach (Fairfax, Virginia: CEEM Information Services, 1994), 141–145.

3. M. Phipps, paper from respondent to ISO/TC 207 and conformity assessment for products presentation; paper presented at ISO/CASCO Conformity Assessment for Environmental Management Workshop, June 12–13, 1995, Geneva, Switzerland.

4. Deloitte Touche Tohmatsu International and Quality Systems Update, *ISO 9000 Survey* (Fairfax, Virginia: CEEM Information Services, September 1993).

5. The RvC in the Netherlands has also accredited registration organizations to offer BS 7750 registrations. Both RvC and UKAS are allowed to accredit non-UK firms that offer BS 7750 certifications. RvC and UKAS are working toward mutual recognition of their certificates. The UKAS is also working with its European counterparts in the European Accreditation of Certification (EAC) to establish a consistent basis for the accreditation of EMAS verifiers on the basis of BS 7750 and ISO 14001.

6. This discussion is based in part on Martin Houldin, "Environmental Management and Conformity Assessment—The BS 7750 Experience," paper presented at ISO/CASCO Conformity Assessment for Environmental Management Workshop, June 12–13, 1995, Geneva, Switzerland.

7. Ronald McLean, paper from respondent to the BS 7750 Experience; paper presented at ISO/CASCO Conformity Assessment for Environmental Management Workshop, June 12–13, 1995, Geneva, Switzerland.

8. Ibid.

Chapter Twelve

ISO 14000 Implementation— Getting Started

Proactive companies all over the world are examining the requirements of ISO 14001 closely. Many are implementing an EMS that will comply with ISO 14001 and making plans for possible registration of their EMS programs. Detailed information about ISO 14001 implementation lies beyond the scope of this book. This chapter will offer a few suggestions, however, in case you're thinking about putting ISO 14000 to work in your organization.

SHOULD YOU SEEK ISO 14001 REGISTRATION?

The ISO 14000 standards can be used as internal tools only. Companies can demonstrate compliance through simple self-declaration, or they can pursue third-party registration. The main reason to implement ISO 14000 is to help your organization handle its environmental responsibilities more effectively. The result? More systematic compliance with requirements (internal or external), better environmental performance, and, possibly, higher profits.

The point is: achieving those goals doesn't require going the extra step of registering your EMS program. Only when you need a clear reason to demonstrate conformance to others does registration become a factor. Some reasons to seek third-party confirmation through registration include:

- Your customers require your EMS to be registered as a condition for signing a contract.
- You're a supplier to a customer that strongly suggests or encourages you to seek registration.

- A government agency either mandates ISO 14001 registration, offers you recognition, or provides some other tangible benefit to ISO 14001-registered companies.
- You have a site(s) in one of the European Union member states, and market pressures or regulatory mandates dictate compliance with the EMAS regulation, possibly using the ISO 14001 route as a strategy.
- You export to markets where ISO 14001 registration becomes a de facto requirement for market entry.
- ISO 14001 registration is likely to offer your organization a competitive advantage in your industry.
- Your major stakeholders, such as your local community, environmental groups, or the public, expect excellent environmental performance, and ISO 14001 may be one way to demonstrate it.

WHICH STANDARD IN THE SERIES?

ISO 14001 is the only standard in the series designed for registration use at this time. Of course, if we're talking about all standards and requirements that can help your EMS efforts, it may also make sense to look at the requirements of EMAS, government regulations and policies related to environmental management and auditing, and any other voluntary initiatives or requirements to which you plan to subscribe.

SCOPE OF THE REGISTRATION

The scope of the registration corresponds to the scope of your EMS, which can cover a particular plant or operations that are part of a site, or comprise several sites. The EMS can also encompass the division or the corporate level. Organizations with ISO 9000 registered sites will likely define the scope of ISO 14000 registration in a similar manner.

Most companies that pursued ISO 9000 registration registered site by site. That way, if a particular plant closed down or for any reason lost its registration, it did not affect the whole system or cause the entire business to lose its registration.

DEVELOPING A SYSTEM

Perhaps the most important yet most basic implementation advice is to develop some kind of organized system. In many companies, bits and pieces of an effective EMS are in place, but they were developed piecemeal in response to new regulations, new products and services, and other developments. Like gears in a transmission that are grinding and haven't yet meshed, they need to be fitted together to form a cohesive whole.

INITIAL ENVIRONMENTAL REVIEW

If you're new to the process, you can benefit from the initial review process described in Annex A to ISO 14001 and in the EMAS regulation. This involves gathering information for a baseline assessment—examining where you are and where you want to go. Your goal is to look at all aspects of your company and identify risks and opportunities, strengths and weaknesses. Areas to look at include:

- Legislative and regulatory requirements.
- Existing environmental management practices and procedures.
- Any existing analysis of significant environmental aspects.
- Existing results of measuring, monitoring, and other types of performance evaluation.
- Feedback from investigation of previous incidents, accidents, and noncompliance with regulations.
- Information from environmental risk assessments.
- Analysis of normal and abnormal operations and emergency conditions.
- The views of relevant interested parties, complaints, and their follow-up.

MANAGEMENT COMMITMENT AND SUPPORT

This point is repeated so often as to be a mantra; commitment and support at the highest levels are absolutely essential to ISO 14000 success. Top management must really believe what it says and put its money where its mouth is.

Support means all resources—time, people, and financial—necessary to do the job. Ideally, it means accountability as well and tangible rewards for effective environmental performance from managers and all employees.

It means rewarding employees for discovering problems and solving them, not for sweeping them under the rug. It also involves rewarding not just for technical compliance but for improved environmental performance through innovative solutions to issues that aren't covered by regulations.

MEASURING COSTS AND BENEFITS

It's easier to measure the costs of environmental performance than its benefits. Any measures that can be used to quantify the short- and long-term benefits of EMS implementation will help you sell ISO 14000 implementation to top management. It will also help the process justify itself and succeed.

The most obvious measures discussed in this book are cost savings due to strategies such as:

- Choosing better alternatives in raw materials and other components from suppliers.
- Substituting less hazardous materials for toxic materials.
- Making efficient use of what were previously waste products.
- Improving plant and office housekeeping through recycling and other methods.

Especially for small and medium-size businesses, it's important to justify ISO 14000 implementation and registration in terms of their return on investment. Too many smaller companies (and plenty of bigger companies) are spending a sizable percentage of operating costs on meeting environmental responsibilities. For these companies, environmental protection is an obstacle, not a business opportunity. Demonstrating to management that EMS adds value will help move the process along.

TC 207 has not yet addressed the concerns of SMEs. Depending on the definition used, small to medium-sized companies constitute anywhere from 75 percent to 90 percent of companies worldwide. Many such companies need more knowledge of environmental issues and the resources for ISO 14000 implementation. The ISO 14004 guidance standard advises SMEs to seek outside help from industry associations, consultants, other companies they work with (such as waste management companies), and similar resources.

ENVIRONMENTAL ASPECTS AND IMPACTS

One of the most important steps in EMS implementation is identifying environmental aspects associated with your activities, processes, and products. The most readily apparent aspects may be those that are regulated, such as emissions to air and water, hazardous materials waste management, and waste disposal. Other aspects include raw material use, packaging, processing energy, and transportation. Many federal and state regulations already dictate the aspects of activities and processes that must be examined.

In examining environmental aspects, another important point is to prioritize those you can control or reasonably influence. The ISO 14004 guidance standard includes some factors to evaluate. A few of these include:

- The scale of the impact.
- Its severity.
- The probability that it may occur.
- How permanent the impact may be.
- Cost of changing the impact.
- Effect of the change on other activities and processes.

OBJECTIVES AND TARGETS

How high do you set your objectives and targets? Sometimes these are set for you by regulatory mandates. In situations where they aren't, you don't have to set unreasonably high objectives and targets just to please an ISO 14000 auditor (e.g., zero pollution within a year). Neither should you set them so low as to question the need for an elaborate EMS in the first place. The standard calls for continual improvement of the EMS to achieve overall improvements in environmental performance.

Many organizations, including SMEs, can use a step-by-step approach to achieving reasonable and incremental targets. If the organization sets targets that it doesn't meet, the real issue for the auditor is not whether any single target has been missed but whether systems are in place that will allow targets to be achieved within reasonable time frames.

PERFORMANCE, NOT BUREAUCRACY

This has been said before but bears repeating: ISO 14001 does not necessarily require either a separate bureaucracy or reams of documentation. Some participants in the process fear that ISO 14001 will require such a burdensome bureaucracy that it will reduce its effectiveness and its acceptance worldwide.

We hope this will not happen. The ultimate aim is an improved EMS system with better environmental results, not an elaborate EMS bureaucracy, complex flow charts of procedures, and a huge manual that decorates a shelf.

The environmental area is already heavily burdened by paperwork and information requirements. The purpose of documentation is to create the discipline of a system and to demonstrate conformance to auditors, not to become an end in itself.

The less additional documentation needed, the better. It may be useful to work with existing documentation and not develop anything new unless absolutely necessary. If you have an ISO 9000 system in place, you can use the same types of procedures and documents for areas common to both ISO 9000 and ISO 14000. These may include document control, inspection and testing procedures. and some process control procedures. It may well be more cost-effective to adapt existing systems than to create entirely new ones.

PROCEED IN STEPS

The ISO 14000 standards suggest, and the experience of many companies confirms, that it's a good idea to proceed in steps. If your organization hasn't addressed any environmental concerns, you don't need to immediately try to make such concerns intrinsic to every part of your operations.

You can focus on the most obvious environmental aspects first and identify those objectives that can be achieved with available resources and those that result in clear business benefits. This includes reducing regulatory violations, saving money through recycling, reducing waste, and similar measures. At this point, you may not attempt to integrate your environmental systems with other business operations. You can pay attention, instead, to putting the most basic elements of ISO 14001 in place.

As awareness of environmental issues develops throughout your organization, as resources become available, as understanding of additional environmental aspects increases, and as information comes in from the measurement system, you can move on to a higher level.

EMPLOYEE EDUCATION AND AWARENESS IS CRITICAL

Another key theme in ISO 14000 is that everyone in the company, to some extent, becomes an environmentalist. The ISO 14000 series is based on a holistic, systems-oriented paradigm of industrial operation. This approach breaks down "turf walls" and gets people from different parts of the company (design, production, quality, environmental health and safety, engineering, housekeeping, etc.) working together. This requires teamwork, cooperation, good communication, and extensive training to acquaint employees with the environmental aspects of their jobs.

CULTURE CHANGE

Many companies that implemented ISO 9000 successfully realized that perhaps the biggest obstacles were not the lack of procedures or technical understanding of the issues but rather the business cultures of the companies themselves. Changing procedures, writing new documentation, or adding a new layer of bureaucracy didn't work (or didn't last long) unless they were accompanied by a cultural change in the way business was perceived.

Just as ISO 9000 companies learned to view their business through the "quality lens," ISO 14000 companies may need to view their activities through the "environmental lens."

Managers familiar with total quality management (TQM) understand the concept of "ownership." The aim is for all employees to own the environmental issues and the environmental aspects of their jobs. In this way, environmental issues become linked with basic business decisions throughout the company.

Cultural change also takes time and effort. If you think you can implement ISO 14000 quickly and then rush out to "buy an ISO 14001 certificate," you may well be disappointed with the lack of a long-term payoff.

CONCLUSION

By this juncture, you should already have some answers to the following two questions: First, what should your organization do about ISO 14000? And second, does ISO 14000 matter?

The first question doesn't have a simple answer. It depends on your organization, the nature of your industry, the demands of the marketplace, the pace and the standards development, the eventual credibility of the conformity assessment infrastructure, and other factors.

At a minimum, it's a good idea to monitor the work of TC 207 and that of other initiatives, such as EMAS. You can influence the development of the standards by getting involved in the standards development process.

If you're interested in developing an EMS system, get a copy of the standards and examine them closely. You may decide to put the standards to work internally, to develop an EMS program, or to improve an existing program. Later, you may want to seek registration to demonstrate to stakeholders that you are a good environmental citizen.

The second question—does ISO 14000 matter?—has a simpler answer: Yes. ISO 14000 is the first international attempt to standardize a systematic approach to environmental management. ISO 14000 is developing a common global language for understanding environmental challenges. It is drawing people together from around the world to tackle complex concepts such as environmental performance evaluation and life cycle assessment, thereby raising the level of knowledge of these issues. It is increasing awareness about the importance of management in promoting better environmental performance. It is highlighting positive alternatives to expensive and complex command-and-control regulations. It is offering incentives to businesses worldwide to take a closer look at the way their activities interact with the environment.

The scope of the standardization effort is far reaching and will touch every aspect of the way industry—in every sector, in companies both large and small—confronts the challenges of environmental protection.

As the pace of industry expands and economic growth surges forward, as population increases, and as resource use begins to strain the carrying capacity of Planet Earth, there is little doubt that the environmental management of industrial operations will play a pivotal role in contributing to sustainable development.

Even though formal publication of the first ISO 14000 standards is still months away, the ISO 14000 movement is here to stay. EMS implementation, whether to ISO 14001 or some other standard, may well become an indispensable tool for those businesses that aim not just to survive but to thrive well into the 21st century.

Matrix Comparison of ISO 14001, EMAS, BS 7750, and ISO 9001 Requirements

ISO/DIS 14001	EMAS (EEC Regulation 1836/93)	BS 7750: 1994	ISO 9001:1994
4.0 General		4.1 Environmental management system	4.2.1 General
ENVIRONMENTAL POLICY 4.1 Environmental policy	Article 3(a) Adopt an environmental policy	4.2 Environmental policy	4.1.1 Quality policy
PLANNING 4.2 Planning			4.2.3 Quality planning
4.2.1 Environmental aspects	Article 3(b) Conduct an environmental review of the site on environmental issues addressed in Annex 1,C	4.4 Environmental effects	
	Annex I,B,3 Environmental effects: Environmental effects evaluation and registration	4.4.2 Environmental effects evaluation and register	

(Continued)

ISO/DIS 14001	EMAS (EEC Regulation 1836/93)	BS 7750: 1994	ISO 9001:1994
4.2.2 Legal and other requirements	Annex I,B,3 Register of legislative, regulatory, and other policy requirements	4.4.3 Register of regulatory, and other policy requirements	4.4.4 Design input (requirements must include applicable statutory and regulatory requirements)
4.2.3 Objectives and targets	Article 3(e) and Annex I, A, 4 Set objectives aimed at continuous improvement of environmental performance and revise the environmental program to achieve them	4.5 Environmental objectives and targets	4.1.1 Policy for quality must include objectives for quality and commitment to quality
4.2.4 Environmental management program	Article 3(c) and Annex I,A,5 Introduce an environmental program and an EMS for the site	4.6 Environmental management program	
IMPLEMENTATION AND OPERATION 4.3.1 Structure and responsibility	Annex I,B,2 Organization and personnel	4.3 Organization and personnel	4.1.2 Organization
4.3.2 Training, awareness, and competence	Annex I,B,2 Organization and personnel: personnel, communications, and training	4.3.4 Personnel, communication, and training	4.18 Training
4.3.3 Communication	Annex I,B,2 Organization and personnel: personnel, communications, and training	4.4.1 Communications	

(Continued)

ISO/DIS 14001	EMAS (EEC Regulation 1836/93)	BS 7750: 1994	ISO 9001:1994
		4.9 Environmental management records (availability of records, both internally and to interested parties)	
4.3.4 Environmental management system documentation	Annex I,B,5 Environmental management documentation records; Annex I,B,4,(a) Requires documented work instructions	4.7 Environmental management manual and documentation 4.7.1 Manual	4.2.1 General (requires documentation of quality system and a quality manual)
4.3.5 Document control	Annex I,B Environmental management documentation records; Establish records to demonstrate compliance with EMS	4.7.2 Documentation	4.5 Document and data control
4.3.6 Operational control	Annex I,B,4 Operational control	4.8 Operational control	4.2.2 Quality system procedures
4.3.6 (c) Procedures related to suppliers and contractors	Annex I,B,4 (b) Operational control; Procedures dealing with procurement and contracted activities	4.3.5 Contractors	4.6 Purchasing 4.7 Control of customer-supplied product
			4.3 Contract review
			4.4 Design control
			4.6 Purchasing
			4.7 Control of customer-supplied product

(Continued)

ISO/DIS 14001	EMAS (EEC Regulation 1836/93)	BS 7750: 1994	ISO 9001:1994
—	—	—	4.9 Process control
—	—	—	4.15 Handling storage, packaging, preservation, and delivery
—	—	—	4.19 Servicing
—	—	—	4.8 Product identification and traceability
4.3.7 Emergency preparedness and response	Annex I,C,9 Prevention and limitation of environmental accidents; 10 Contingency procedures in cases of environmental accidents	4.4.2 Environmental effects evaluation and register, procedures to include consideration of incidents, accidents, and potential emergency situations (Paragraph 3)	
CHECKING AND CORRECTIVE ACTION			
4.4.1 Monitoring and measurement	Annex I,B,5 Operational control; Monitoring	4.8.3 Verification, measurement, and testing	4.10 Inspection and testing
			4.12 Inspection and test status
			4.20 Statistical techniques
			4.11 Control of inspection, measurement, and test equipment
4.4.2 Nonconformance and corrective and preventive action	Annex I,B,4 Operational control; Noncompliance and corrective action	4.8.4 Noncompliance and corrective action	4.13 Control of nonconforming product

(Continued)

ISO/DIS 14001	EMAS (EEC Regulation 1836/93)	BS 7750: 1994	ISO 9001:1994
			4.14 Corrective and preventive action
4.4.3 Records	Annex I,B,5 Environmental management documentation records	4.9 Environmental management records	4.16 Control of quality records
4.4.4 Environmental management system audit	Article 3(d) Carry out or cause to be carried out environmental audits at the sites concerned, in accordance with Article 4 (Article 4 describes the details of the auditing and validation process); Annex I,B,6 Environmental audits	4.10 Environmental management audits 4.10.1 General 4.10.2 Audit program 4.10.3 Audit protocols and procedcures	4.17 Internal quality audits
MANAGEMENT REVIEW			
4.5 Management review	Article 3(e) and Annex I,B,1 Revise the policy and EMS in accordance with audit findings and revise objectives, aimed at continuous improvement of environmental performance	4.11 Environmental management reviews	4.1.3 Management review
	Article 3(f) Prepare an environmental statement specific to each site audited		
	Article 3(g) Verify the EMS and the statement; Validate the environmental statement		

(Continued)

ISO/DIS 14001	EMAS (EEC Regulation 1836/93)	BS 7750: 1994	ISO 9001:1994
	Article 3(h) Forward the validated environmental statement to the competent body of the member state where the site is located and disseminate it as appropriate to the public		

Eco-Management and Audit Scheme Requirements

EMAS consists of 21 Articles and 5 Annexes.

DEFINITIONS

Article 2 contains definitions for key terms. A few of these include the following.

Environmental Review

This means "an initial comprehensive analysis of the environmental issues, impacts, and performance related to a site."

Company

Company refers to the "organization which has overall management control over activities at a given site." This may be more site specific than the reference in 14001.

Site

A site according to EMAS refers to "all land on which the industrial activity under the control of a company at a given location is carried out." EMAS is more site-specific than the ISO 14000's reference to organization.

Environmental Statement

This is a statement prepared by the company that is validated by the EMAS verifier. A publicly distributed and verified environmental statement is not required by ISO 14001; this is a key difference between the two systems.

DETAILED REQUIREMENTS

The detailed requirements of EMAS start with Article 3.

Environmental Policy

The company environmental policy, and the EMS program for the site, must be established in writing, adopted, periodically reviewed in light of environmental audits by management, and revised, as appropriate. The policy must be communicated to the company's personnel and be available to the public.

The EMAS regulation states that the environmental policy must be based on the following set of principles:

- Foster a sense of responsibility for the environment among employees at all levels.
- Assess the environmental impact of all new activities, products, and processes in advance.
- Assess and monitor the impact of current activities on the local environment. It must examine the significant impact of these activities on the environment in general.
- Take measures necessary to prevent or eliminate pollution, and where this is not feasible, reduce pollutant emissions and waste generation to a minimum and conserve resources. These measures shall take into account possible clean technologies.
- Take measures necessary to prevent accidental emissions of materials or energy.
- Establish and apply monitoring procedures to check compliance with the environmental policy. Where these procedures require measurement and testing, the company shall establish and update records of the results.
- Establish and update procedures and actions to be pursued if the company detects noncompliance with its environmental policy, objectives, or targets.
- Cooperate with the public authorities to establish and update contingency procedures to minimize the impact of any accidental discharges to the environment.
- Provide to the public information necessary to understand the environmental impact of the company's activities and pursue an open dialogue with the public.

- Provide appropriate advice to customers on the relevant environmental aspects of the handling, use, and disposal of its products. (Note: ISO 14001 doesn't provide explicit requirements to provide advice to customers.)
- Make sure that contractors working at the site on the company's behalf apply environmental standards equivalent to those of the company.

Issues the Policy and Program Must Address

The environmental policy, program, and environmental audits must address the following 12 issues:

1. Assessment, control, and reduction of the impact of the activity concerned on the various sectors of the environment.
2. Energy management, savings, and choice.
3. Raw materials management, savings, choice, and transportation; water management and savings.
4. Waste avoidance, recycling, reuse, transportation, and disposal.
5. Evaluation, control, and reduction of noise within and outside the site.
6. Selection of new production processes and changes to production processes.
7. Product planning (design, packaging, transportation, use, and disposal).
8. Environmental performance and practices of contractors, subcontractors, and suppliers.
9. Prevention and limitation of environmental accidents.
10. Contingency procedures for environmental accidents.
11. Staff information and training on environmental issues.
12. External information on environmental issues.

Environmental Objectives

EMAS requires the company to specify environmental objectives at all relevant levels within the company and quantify wherever practical its commitment to continual improvement in environmental performance over defined time scales.

Conduct an Environmental Review

EMAS calls for an initial environmental review that focuses on the 12 areas described above.

Introduce an Environmental Program and EMS

The environmental program and EMS must be applicable to all activities at the site. It must designate responsibility for objectives at each function and level of the company and describe the means by which they are to be achieved.

EMAS also calls for separate programs relating to new or modified products, services, or processes. The programs must define:

- The environmental objectives to achieve.
- How to achieve them.
- Procedures for dealing with changes and modifications as projects proceed.
- Corrective mechanisms to employ if the need arises, how to activate them, and how to measure their adequacy in particular situations.

The specific elements of an EMS program required by EMAS include the following:

- Establish, review, and revise its policy, objectives, and programs for the site.
- Define and document the responsibility, authority, and inter-relations of key personnel who manage, perform, and monitor work affecting the environment.
- Appoint a management representative who has authority and responsibility for ensuring that the management system is implemented and maintained.
- Ensure that employees understand the importance of complying with EMS requirements, are aware of the environmental effects of their work, understand their roles and responsibilities, and know the consequences of violating procedures.
- Identify training needs and provide appropriate training.
- Establish and maintain procedures for receiving, documenting, and responding to communications, both internal and external,

from relevant interested parties concerning its environmental effects and management.

- Examine its environmental effects and compile a register of significant effects.
- Establish operating procedures to plan and control activities and processes that affect or potentially affect the environment.
- Develop documented work instructions that define the work of employees and others acting on the company's behalf.
- Develop procurement/contracting procedures to ensure that suppliers and those acting on their behalf comply with the company's policies.
- Monitor and control relevant process characteristics (such as effluent streams and waste disposal).
- Monitor each activity, including establishing and maintaining records of the results.
- Investigate and correct noncompliances with environmental policies, objectives, and standards.
- Apply controls to ensure that preventive actions are effective and record changes in procedures that result from corrective action.
- Establish documentation that describes its policies, objectives, and programs, the key roles and responsibilities of personnel, and the interactions of the EMS system elements.
- Establish records to demonstrate compliance with the requirements of the environmental management system and to record the extent to which planned environmental objectives have been met.
- Set up, implement, and revise a systematic and periodic program of environmental audits.

Environmental Effects Register

EMAS requires the company to compile a register of significant environmental effects. The register must consider, where appropriate:

1. Controlled and uncontrolled emissions to atmosphere.
2. Controlled and uncontrolled discharges to water or sewers.
3. Solid and other wastes, particularly hazardous wastes.
4. Contamination of land.

5. Use of land, water, fuels and energy, and other natural resources.

6. Discharge of thermal energy, noise, odor, dust, vibration, and visual impact.

7. Effects on specific parts of the environment and ecosystems. This includes effects arising or likely to arise, due to:

   a. Normal operating conditions.

   b. Abnormal operating conditions.

   c. Incidents, accidents, and potential emergency situations.

   d. Past activities, current activities, and planned activities.

Conduct Environmental Auditing

EMAS calls for the organization to set up, implement, and revise a systematic and periodic program of environmental audits concerning:

- Whether or not the environmental management activities conform to the environmental program and are implemented effectively.
- How effective the EMS is in fulfilling the company's environmental policy.

It must then carry out or cause to be carried out environmental audits at the site. The audits may be conducted by either company auditors or external auditors acting on the company's behalf. The criteria for the auditing are the same 12 issues mentioned above. The audit checks to make sure the 12 issues were addressed by the EMS program.

EMAS requires the audit frequency (the audit cycle) to be completed at intervals of no longer than three years. Top management decides the frequency of the audits for each activity at the site, taking into account the following:

- Potential overall environment impact of the activities at the site.
- Nature, scale, and complexity of the activities.
- Nature and scale of emissions, waste raw material, and energy consumption and, in general, the nature and scale of the activity's interaction with the environment.
- Importance and urgency of the problems detected following the initial environmental review or the previous audit.
- History of environmental problems.

Set High Objectives and Revise the Program

Based on its audit findings, the company must set objectives at the highest appropriate management level "aimed at the continuous improvement of environmental performance," and it must revise the environmental program to be able to achieve the objectives.

The Environmental Statement

The company must prepare an environmental statement specific to each site audited when the initial environmental review and subsequent audits or audit cycles are completed. The first such environmental statement must include the following information:

- Description of the site's activities.
- An assessment of all significant environmental issues relevant to the activities at the site.
- Summary of figures on pollution emissions, waste production, consumption of raw material, energy, and water, and noise and other significant and appropriate environmental aspects.
- Other factors regarding environmental performance.
- Presentation of the environmental policy, program, and the management system implemented at the site.
- Deadline for submission of the next statement.
- Name of the accredited environmental verifier.
- Significant changes since the previous statement.

Verification and Validation

The company must have its system examined by an external accredited verifier and its environmental statement validated to ensure that they meet the requirements of EMAS. The verifier checks whether:

- The environmental policy has been established and whether it meets the requirements of EMAS.
- An EMS is in place at the site, in operation, and complies with relevant EMAS requirements.
- The environmental review and audit are carried out in accordance with EMAS requirements.

- The data and information in the environmental statement are reliable and whether the statement adequately covers all the significant and relevant environmental issues. If so, the statement is validated.

The regulation includes a nondisclosure clause. The auditors and verifiers can't divulge, without authorization from company management, any information or data obtained in the course of their activities.

This nondisclosure clause takes precedence over any national law in place in the various member states—in practice a number of the member states have laws which would normally require a verifier/auditor to inform the authorities if they discovered a breach of law during the course of their work. This requirement of EMAS ensures that the prior authorization of the management of the site must be obtained before any disclosure is made when the verifier/auditor is working as part of an EMAS implementation.

The First Verification and Validation

The verifier can encounter two situations when performing the first verification and validation: the site may already have a well-developed, operating EMS in place, or the site may have just implemented a new EMS. In the first situation, the verifier checks compliance by examining the initial review, any internal audit, and other internal monitoring procedures. In the second situation, the focus is on the initial environmental review, its organization, execution, and results.

A guidance document published by the European Commission to the verification and validation process points out that verification does not involve value judgments of the specific policy objectives, performance targets, and standards established by the company itself, but is only a check to ensure that these are in conformity with the regulation.

The verifier checks to make sure the company's policy is in compliance with all the relevant requirements of the regulation, including (and in particular) commitments aimed at reasonable continuous environmental improvement. The verifier will not independently assess environmental impacts and issues. That's the company's job, as part of its environmental review.

Site Registration

Site registration occurs when the competent body, designated by the member state, receives a validated environmental statement, levies a registration fee, and is satisfied the site meets the regulation's requirements, including complying with all relevant environmental legislation.

A site can lose its registration in the EMAS scheme under the following conditions:

- If it fails to submit a validated environmental statement and registration fee within three months of the deadline specified in its previous statement.
- If a competent body becomes aware that the site is no longer in compliance with the requirements of the regulation.
- If an enforcement authority informs a competent body that the site is no longer in compliance with relevant environmental legislation.

Appendix C

US Government Auditing and Enforcement Policies

This appendix looks at the question: If a company engages in auditing, whether compliance or EMS auditing, what will the US government's response be? As a corollary, what incentives will the US government offer for companies that engage in auditing and other self-evaluative activities along the lines described in ISO 14001?

ISO 14001 is based partly on the notion that what you know can only help you improve. On the other hand, many companies that now engage in self-evaluative activities (such as auditing) are concerned about the enforcement consequences. They're operating on an opposite assumption, that what you know can hurt you, especially if the government finds out. If you stay ignorant, you will ignore problems that may bring on enforcement actions. But if you audit thoroughly and disclose the results, you may get hit even harder. In too many companies, the results are often no audits, audits with a narrowly defined scope, or audits with sanitized reports that end up misleading management.

Many in US industry have been calling for more assurance that self-evaluative information used to identify and correct problems would not be used against the company by the government or for some kind of "safe harbor" from penalty impositions. Thus, the government's stance toward auditing is an important consideration for companies considering ISO 14000 registration.

The following is a description of US government policies regarding auditing, primarily those of the EPA and Department of Justice (DOJ).

EPA 1986 AUDITING POLICY

The first formal policy by EPA regarding voluntary auditing came in its 1986 auditing policy.[1] This policy has been recently updated and changed.

The 1986 policy includes a description of the elements of an effective auditing policy. The 1986 policy and the draft 1995 policy include the following key points.

The EPA Favors Auditing

In general, the EPA favors voluntary auditing as a very useful way for companies to achieve compliance and improve performance. It doesn't seek to mandate auditing or dictate methods that companies follow. In general, it acknowledges the importance of voluntary auditing as an alternative to costly "command-and-control" regulation.

No Routine Requests, but Discretion Remains

The EPA will not routinely request environmental audit reports. When companies take action to avoid incidents of noncompliance, quickly correct environmental problems discovered through audits, and implement preventive measures, the EPA may consider such actions as honest and genuine efforts to assure compliance. It will take these efforts into account when setting inspection priorities and in fashioning enforcement responses to violations. To the extent that compliance performance is considered in setting inspection priorities, facilities with a good compliance history may be subject to fewer inspections.

The EPA, however, retains its discretion on a case-by-case basis to accomplish a statutory mission or where the material is necessary for a criminal investigation. It won't promise to forgo inspections, reduce enforcement responses, or offer other such incentives in exchange for implementation of environmental auditing or other sound environmental management practices. In short, auditing is valuable but not an alternative to regulatory oversight.

Reports Can't Shield Information

The EPA acknowledges the importance of self-evaluation and the need for privacy. But audit reports can't shield monitoring, compliance, or other information that would otherwise be reportable and/or accessible to the EPA, even if there is no explicit requirement to generate that data.

Audit Provisions as Remedies in Enforcement Actions

The EPA may propose environmental auditing provisions in consent decrees and in other settlement negotiations where auditing could provide a remedy for identified problems and reduce the likelihood of similar problems recurring in the future. In its policy on inclusion of environmental auditing provisions in such settlements ("EPA Policy on the Inclusion of Environmental Auditing Provisions in Enforcement Settlements"), it describes two types of audits—compliance and management. The management audit is essentially what ISO 14000 envisions as an EMS audit, and the compliance audit could be the type used by companies to evaluate compliance to legal requirements.

EPA'S 1995 DRAFT INTERIM AUDITING POLICY

In March 1995, the EPA revised its auditing policy by issuing a draft interim policy. Although the policy doesn't satisfy everyone in industry, it offers more enforcement certainty. Here are the key provisions of the proposed policy.

Eliminate or Reduce Penalties

First, the agency will completely eliminate the "gravity" component of civil penalties[2] for companies that voluntarily identify, disclose, and correct violations according to certain conditions. The exceptions are violations involving criminal conduct by the company or any of its employees, repeat violations, or violations that pose danger or harm to human health or the environment. The EPA will also reduce punitive penalties by up to 75 percent for companies that meet most, but not all, of the conditions.

The agency would still collect economic benefits derived from noncompliance to make sure violators do not gain a competitive advantage through noncompliance. However, the EPA may forgive the entire penalty for violations that meet the conditions outlined in the policy and, in the EPA's discretion, do not merit any penalty due to the insignificant amount of any economic benefit.

Voluntary Environmental Self-Policing and Self-Disclosure Interim Policy Statement—Conditions

To receive the policy's benefits, a company must meet the following conditions:

1. It discovers the violation through a voluntary environmental audit or voluntary self-evaluation appropriate to its size and nature.

2. It voluntarily discloses the violation fully in writing to all appropriate federal, state, and local agencies as soon as it is discovered and before the:

   a. Start of a federal, state, or local agency inspection, investigation, or information request.

   b. Notice of a citizen suit.

   c. Legal complaint by a third party.

   d. The company's knowledge that discovery of the violation was imminent by a regulatory agency or third party.

3. The company corrects the violation either within 60 days or as expeditiously as practical.

4. The company quickly remedies any condition that created or may create dangers to human health or the environment.

5. The company remedies any environmental harm and acts to prevent a recurrence.

6. The violation must not indicate a failure to take appropriate steps to avoid repeat or recurring violations.

7. The company cooperates fully with the EPA in providing information, including entering into a written agreement, administrative consent order, or judicial consent decree.

Limit Criminal Referrals

EPA also intends to provide greater certainty as to how it will exercise investigative discretion. The agency will not refer cases involving companies that voluntarily disclose and promptly correct violations to the Department of Justice (DOJ) for criminal prosecution. The exceptions include criminal acts of managers or employees, cases where violations are concealed or condoned, where there's conscious involvement and willful blindness to violations, or where there's serious actual harm to the environment.

No Requests for Audit

In its new policy, the EPA emphasizes that it will not request voluntary environmental audit reports to trigger a civil or criminal investigation, but only where it has independent information that indicates a violation may have occurred.

DEPARTMENT OF JUSTICE POLICY

The Department of Justice has also published guidance that is relevant to the development of EMS programs. In 1991, the DOJ published guidance for prosecutors to assist them in making decisions regarding criminal prosecutions for environmental violations.[3] The key points in this policy include the following.

Voluntary Auditing Is a Mitigating Factor

The DOJ's policy is to encourage self-auditing, self-policing, and voluntary disclosure of environmental violations by indicating that these activities are viewed as mitigating factors when deciding between civil or criminal enforcement. Basically, a good management system may decrease the chances of criminal prosecution. The factors that the DOJ takes into consideration when considering whether and how to prosecute are listed below. If a company fully meets all of the criteria, the result may be a decision not to prosecute that company criminally. Even it doesn't meet all the criteria, the company can benefit from some degree of enforcement response by the government.

DOJ'S MITIGATING FACTORS

1. **Voluntary disclosure.** Has the regulated entity made a "voluntary, timely, and complete disclosure of the matter under investigation"? This means a disclosure that occurred before "a law enforcement or regulatory authority had already obtained

knowledge regarding noncompliance. A disclosure is not considered to be voluntary if that disclosure is already specifically required by law, regulation, or permit."

2. **Cooperation.** Was cooperation by the violator full and prompt? This include a "willingness to make all relevant information (including the complete results of any internal or external investigation and the names of all potential witnesses) available to government investigators and prosecutors."

3. **Preventive measures and compliance programs.** The attorney for the Department should consider the existence and scope of any regularized, intensive, and comprehensive environmental compliance program; such a program may include an environmental compliance or management audit.

Additional factors that may be relevant

4. **Pervasiveness of noncompliance.**
5. **Existence of internal disciplinary action.**
6. **Subsequent compliance efforts to remedy any ongoing noncompliance.**

US SENTENCING COMMISSION GUIDELINES

In 1991, the US Sentencing Commission issued *Organization Sentencing Guidelines,* which also encourage companies to implement systematic environmental audit programs, to report detected violations, and to cooperate affirmatively with government investigators.[4]

If an organization has implemented such programs, it can receive a substantial reduction in its scheduled sentence under the sentencing guidelines. The guidelines state that an effective compliance program is one that is "reasonably designed, implemented, and enforced so that it generally will be effective in preventing and detecting criminal conduct."

In 1993, the Sentencing Commission published its *Draft Corporate Sentencing Guidelines for Environmental Violations,* prepared by the US Sentencing Commission's Advisory Group on Environmental Sanctions. In *Paragraph 9C1.2, Mitigating factors in sentence, paragraph (a),* the proposal mentions commitment to environmental compliance. In *Part D— Commitment to environmental compliance, Section 9D1.1, factors for environmental compliance,* the guidelines trace the outlines for an effective compliance program and describe the key minimum factors demonstrating a commitment to environmental compliance. These are described below.

The guideline recommends that companies get a sentence reduced by up to 50 percent for having an environmental management and compliance program in place. Companies would get credit for the extent to which they have implemented incentives and awards for environmental achievement.

MITIGATING FACTORS IN SENTENCING GUIDELINES

The following are the mitigating factors recommended in the guidelines spelled out in more detail. You'll recognize most of these as essential elements in an effective EMS program.

1. **Line management attention to compliance.** Line managers at every level work at measuring, maintaining, and improving the organization's compliance with environmental laws and regulations. Line managers routinely review environmental monitoring and auditing reports, direct the resolution of identified compliance issues, and ensure application of the resources and mechanisms necessary to carry out a substantial commitment.

2. **Integration of environmental policies, standards, and procedures.** The organization has adopted and communicated to its employees and agents the policies, standards, and procedures necessary to achieve environmental compliance, including a requirement that employees report any suspected violation to appropriate officials within the organization and that a record be kept by the organization of any such reports.

3. **Auditing, monitoring, reporting, and tracking systems.** The organization has designed and implemented, with sufficient authority personnel and other resources:

   a. Frequent auditing and inspection of principal operations.

   b. Continuous on-site monitoring of key operations and pollution control facilities.

    c. Internal reporting of potential noncompliance.

    d. Tracking the status of responses to identified compliance issues to enable expeditious, effective, and documented resolution of environmental compliance issues by line management.

    e. Redundant, independent checks on the status of compliance.

4. **Regulatory expertise, training, and evaluation.** The organization has developed and implemented adequate systems or programs to maintain up-to-date, sufficiently detailed understanding of all applicable environmental requirements. It has evaluated and documented the training and evaluation of all employees and agents of the organization as to the applicable environmental requirements to carry out their responsibilities. And it has evaluated employees and agents sufficiently to avoid delegating authority or unsupervised responsibility to persons who may engage in illegal activities.

5. **Incentives for compliance.** The organization has implemented a system of incentives to reward and recognize employees for their contributions to environmental excellence.

6. **Disciplinary procedures.** The organization has consistently and visibly enforced its environmental policies, standards, and procedures in response to infractions.

7. **Continuing evaluation and improvement.** The organization has implemented a process for measuring its efforts to achieve environmental excellence and for making appropriate improvements or adjustments. If appropriate to the size and nature of the organization, this should include a periodic, external evaluation of the organization's overall compliance effort, as reflected in these factors.

8. **Additional innovative approaches.** This refers to additional programs or components that the organization can show are effective and important to carrying out its overall commitment to environmental compliance.

The guideline recommends that companies get a sentence reduced by up to 90 percent for having an environmental management and compliance program in place. Companies would get credit for the extent to which they have implemented incentives and awards for environmental achievement.

NOTES

1. *Restatement of Policies Related to Environmental Auditing,* EPA Notice, *Federal Register* 59, no. 144 (July 28, 1994), p. 38455–60; *Environmental Auditing Policy Statement,* EPA, *Final Policy Statement, Federal Register* 51, no. 131, (July 9, 1986), pp. 25004ff.

2. The gravity component of a civil penalty is based on the potential for harm and the extent of deviation from a statutory or regulatory requirement.

3. "Factors in Decisions on Criminal Prosecutions for Environmental Violations in the Context of Significant Voluntary Compliance or Disclosure Efforts by the Violator," July 1, 1991.

4. 56 Fed. Reg. 22, 762, Section 8A1.2 Comment K.

Contacts

American National Standards Institute (ANSI)

11 West 42nd Street
New York, New York 10036
Ph: 212–642–4900; Fax: 212–398–0023
Internet: http://www.ansi.org

ANSI is a nonprofit organization that coordinates the U.S. voluntary standards system and develops a wide variety of U.S. consensus standards. It is also the official U.S. member of ISO and IEC. The ISO 14000 standards are available for purchase through ANSI.

The American Society for Quality Control (ASQC)

611 East Wisconsin Avenue
PO Box 3005
Milwaukee, Wisconsin 53201
Ph: 414–272–8575, 800–248–1946; Fax: 414–272–1734

ASQC is a professional not-for-profit association of quality professionals dedicated to developing, promoting and applying quality concepts and methods. Along with ASTM, ASQC administers the US Technical Advisory Group (TAG) to TC 207 and will co-sponsor the American version of the ISO 14000 standards when published.

The American Society for Testing and Materials (ASTM)

1916 Race Street
Philadelphia, Pennsylvania 19103
Ph: 215–299–5400; Fax: 215–299–2630

ASTM develops and publishes voluntary industry standards, tests, practices, guides and definitions for materials, products, systems and services in a variety of industries. These serve as the basis for trade agreements and regulations. ASTM also publishes books describing state-of-the-art testing techniques and their applications. Along with ASQC, ASTM administers the US TAG to TC 207.

Canadian Standards Association (CSA)

178 Rexdale Boulevard
Etobicoke, Ontario
M9W 1R3
Canada
Ph: 416–747–4000; Fax: 416–747–4149

The Canadian Standards Association is an independent, not-for-profit organization dedicated to developing consensus standards and related certification, testing and quality registration programs. CSA is the Secretariat for TC 207.

International Organization for Standardization (ISO)

1, rue de Varembe
Case postale 50
CH-1211
Geneva 20
Switzerland
Ph: 41–22–749–0111; Fax: 41–22–733–3430
Internet: http://www.iso.ch
email: central@isocs.iso.ch

ISO is a worldwide federation of national standards bodies dedicated to developing and promoting international standards with the goal of facilitating the exchange of goods and services. ISO will publish the ISO 14000 series of environmental management standards.

NSF International

3475 Plymouth Road
P.O. Box 130140
Ann Arbor, Michigan 48113-0140
Ph: 313–769–8010, 800–673–6275; Fax: 313–769–0109

NSF International is a not-for-profit organization devoted to research, education and service in the areas of health and the environment. It develops standards and criteria for equipment, products and services related to health. NSF conducts research, and tests and evaluates equipment, products and services for compliance with NSF standards and criteria. Along with ASQC and ANSI, NSF will co-sponsor the American version of the ISO 14000 standards.

References

Environmental Management in a Global Economy. 1994 Conference Proceedings. Arlington, VA: Global Environmental Management Initiative, March 16–17, 1994.

Fischer, Kurt, and Johan Schot. *Environmental Strategies for Industry: International Perspectives on Research Needs and Policy Implications.* Washington, DC: Island Press, 1993.

Friedman, Frank. *Practical Guide to Environmental Management,* 6th ed. Washington, DC: Environmental Law Institute, 1995.

Hunter, Roszell D. "EU Eco-Management and Auditing Regulation: Analysis and Perspective." *BNA International Environmental Reporter*, February 9, 1994, pp. 142–49.

_____. "Standardization and the Environment: Analysis and Perspective." *BNA International Environmental Reporter,* March 19, 1993, pp. 185–91.

Marguglio, B. W. *Environmental Management Systems.* New York: Marcel Dekker; Milwaukee: ASQC Press, 1991.

Peach, Robert W., ed. *The ISO 9000 Handbook,* 2nd ed. Fairfax, VA: CEEM Information Services, 1994.

Society of Environmental Toxicology and Chemistry. *A Technical Framework for Life-Cycle Assessment.* Workshop Report. SETAC Foundation, 1990.

US Environmental Protection Agency. *Evaluation of Environmental Marketing Terms in the United States.* Washington, DC: US Government Printing Office, February 1993.

_____. *Pollution Prevention in the Federal Government: Guide for Developing Pollution Prevention Strategies for Executive Order 12856 and Beyond.* Washington, DC: US Government Printing Office, April 1994.

_____. *The Use of Life Cycle Assessment in Environmental Labeling.* Washington, DC: US Government Printing Office, September 1993.

Willig, John T., ed. *Environmental TQM,* 2nd ed. New York: McGraw-Hill, Inc., 1994.

Wilson, Peter. *The Community Eco-Management and Audit Scheme—An Overview, Progress to Date, and Current Issues.* European Commission, Document EC DG XI.C.5. January 1995.

Index

Other books of interest to you from Irwin Professional Publishing . . .

IMPLEMENTING AN ENVIRONMENTAL AUDIT

How to Gain a Competitive Advantage Using Quality and Environmental Responsibility

Grant Ledgerwood, Elizabeth Street, and Riki Therivel

A unique manual which provides clear, practical guidelines to implementing an effective corporate environmental program. Gives tools to help managers lead their organizations to compliance with environmental regulations by integrating a total quality "green strategy" into the corporate culture.

0-7863-0142-2   225 pages

THE HANDBOOK OF ENVIRONMENTALLY CONSCIOUS MANUFACTURING

From Design & Production to Labeling & Recycling

Robert E. Cattanach, Jake M. Holdreith, Daniel P. Reinke, and Larry K. Sibik

Companies seeking a competitive advantage are employing environmentally responsible design and production methods to meet the demands of their stakeholders, which include customers, regulators, employees, and the community. Gives examples of successful companies which have integrated environmental considerations into the manufacturing process.

0-7863-0147-3   600 pages

THE ISO 9000 HANDBOOK, SECOND EDITION

Edited by Robert W. Peach

This is an extraordinarily detailed, timely, and easy-to-use resource which provides an in-depth, clause-by-clause explanation of the Q9000 series text. Walks the reader through all phases of implementation, and examines the broader issues of product liability, conformity, assessment, and registrar accreditation.

0-883337-31-3   700 pages

About the Authors

TOM TIBOR is a business, technical, and management writer and has written for government, associations, and private industry. He served as Director of Special Projects for CEEM, Inc., publishers of the ISO 9000 newsletter, *Quality Systems Update,* (now published by Irwin Professional Publishing) where he developed and edited several regulatory and standards publications including *The ISO 9000 Handbook, The ISO 9000 Registered Company Directory, European Community Medical Device Directives,* and *European Community Product Liability and Product Safety Directives.* Mr. Tibor is a member of the U.S. Technical Advisory Group (TAG) to ISO Technical Committee 207 on environmental management, and reports on ISO 14000 developments for business and environmental publications.

IRA FELDMAN is Vice President of Capital Environmental, the environmental consulting affiliate of the Howrey & Simon law firm. Until recently, Mr. Feldman served as Special Counsel in the Office of Compliance at EPA headquarters in Washington, D.C., where he developed the Environmental Leadership Program and led the revision of EPA's auditing policy. Mr. Feldman is active in the national and international voluntary standards-setting arena through his participation in the ASTM and ISO processes. He attended the 1995 TC 207 international meeting in Oslo, Norway as the lead U.S. delegate to Subcommittee 6 (Terms and Definitions). The U.S. TAG has designated Mr. Feldman as co-chair of its Legal Issues Forum. He is a member of the board of directors of the Institute for Environmental Auditing and of the editorial board of Total Environmental Quality Management.